TEACHING PORTFOLIOS

Presenting Your Professional Best

Patricia L. Rieman
Northern Illinois University

Boston   Burr Ridge, IL Dubuque, IA Madison, WI New York San Francisco St. Louis
Bangkok Bogotá Caracas Lisbon London Madrid
Mexico City Milan New Delhi Seoul Singapore Sydney Taipei Toronto

McGraw-Hill Higher Education

*A Division of The **McGraw-Hill** Companies*

Teaching Portfolios: Presenting Your Professional Best
Patricia L. Rieman

Published by McGraw-Hill Higher Education, an imprint of The McGraw-Hill Companies, Inc.,
1221 Avenue of the Americas, New York, NY 10020. Copyright © 2000 by The McGraw-Hill
Companies, Inc. All rights reserved.

 This book is printed on recycled, acid-free paper containing 10% postconsumer waste.

4 5 6 7 8 9 0 QPD QPD 0 3 2 1

ISBN 0-07-239093-X

www.mhhe.com

Table of Contents

From the Author

Dear Reader:

I wish I had known back in 1982 when I was interviewing for my first teaching job all that I know now!

On my first interview for a special education position in a small town near Tulsa, Oklahoma, I dressed in "my best," which, unfortunately, was a spaghetti strap sundress with a matching jacket. No portfolio in hand, no hose, for that matter, and to top it off, I was SO SICK! I had a horrid, painful ear infection and was on strong medication. Evidently, I was too sick to even consider the rational approach of rescheduling the interview--I am chagrined to admit that I even used the words, "I'm on drugs right now…" Needless to say, I did not get the job!

Seventeen years later, here I am: a 16 year veteran educator with a Master's in Behavior Disorders, working full-time on my Ed.D. in Curriculum and Instruction at Northern Illinois University and teaching two sections of courses to future educators. I always was a late bloomer…

You will undoubtedly do better than I on those first interviews—not only would it be difficult to have a worse first interview, but the fact that you are reading this booklet and planning ahead by creating a professional portfolio already shows your initiative and know-how. You are using resources to give your best effort to this exciting phase of your career. Be prepared with your portfolio in hand, be wise, be enthusiastic, be eager to learn, show your love for your subject and your students, and show your willingness to work with your team to do what's best for the students.

Best wishes, and welcome to the field!

Sincerely,

Patricia L. Rieman
Northern Illinois University

Dedicated to my husband-the-teacher,
and to all those future teachers in
CIRE 100 and 340, 1999
--thanks for the artifacts and the inspiration!

Preface

Why This Handbook?

Teacher education programs across the nation are encouraging their education majors to begin early the process of documenting their experiences with schools and children. Portfolios are excellent tools for maintaining records, showing growth, and displaying experiences related to the field of education. Students may be assessed with portfolios in their courses, some states are moving toward portfolio documentation requirements for certification, and many administrators appreciate having portfolios to examine when considering candidates for teaching positions.

In an effort to meet the growing need for guidance in how to create portfolios that best portray the abilities of students and new teachers, I offer you my interpretation of current trends and theories in portfolio development. I've researched current documents, texts, and Web sites, and have met with a diverse group of students, principals, and parents to provide a current, balanced view on what artifacts are most valuable in portfolios.

The Handbook's Approach and Organization

Teaching Portfolios: Presenting Your Professional Best is designed to complement any pre-service educational course. Specifically written for pre-service teachers, each chapter begins with either student-generated artifacts or insights from an administrator about what's important in an interview, and then goes on to suggest artifacts for inclusion in a portfolio. Another component of this text is the inclusion of questions for reflection. It is periodically suggested throughout the text that the reader use the note pages at the end of each chapter to pause and write responses to the readings. Also note-worthy is the special care taken to address issues of diversity through sections on curricular modifications, standards, and pro-active classroom management.

Teaching Portfolios: Presenting Your Professional Best is divided into two parts. The first part, <u>Your Portfolio and its Contents</u>, presents what a portfolio is, why it is important, what it should include, how to construct it, and how to organize it based on state, national, or content-area standards. By focusing on the need to reflect, the second part, <u>Presenting Your Professional Best</u>, discusses areas for which the portfolio can be used to illustrate and highlight proficiency. It expands on "what should be in a portfolio" to include guidance on how to make each artifact the best example possible.

Special Features

Pedagogically, depth is added to the handbook through:

- **From The Real World**, a feature that offers words of wisdom (and interview suggestions) from experienced administrators
- **Real artifact examples** provided to guide students in their decisions regarding what to include in their portfolios

- **Annotated Web sites and references**
- **Opportunities for reflection** with special areas designated for note-taking

Key content that pre-service teachers will find invaluable includes:

- A **Portfolio checklist** providing guidance on what should be included in a portfolio
- **How to organize a portfolio around any set of standards** that uses the INTASC Standards as an example
- Information on **Digital Portfolios**
- An **explanation of the importance of portfolios** both in teacher and career development, and the interview process
- **Why reflection is important**
- **How to illustrate your ability to meet individual needs through curricular modifications** in your portfolio
- An **Appendix listing state boards of education and professional organizations**

Acknowledgements

A special thanks is extending to the professors and instructors who provided feedback on this portfolio handbook during its development:

Janet Bliss, Colby-Sawyer College
Jenny O. Burson, University of Texas, Austin
Terrence Caselnova, St. Leo University
Isolete De Almeida, Cameron University
Annette Digby, University of Arkansas
Ruth Ledbetter Gálaz, Western New Mexico University
Linda J. McKinney, University of Oklahoma
Stephen R. Madigosky, Widener University
Dalphia Pierce, University of Scranton
George Rogers, University of Nebraska, Lincoln
Barbara K. Strassman, The College of New Jersey
Sharon Thomas, Miami-Dade Community College
Daniel Thompson, University of Illinois – Urbana-Champaign
Frances van Tassell, University of North Texas
Joan L. Whitman, Cardinal Stritch University

PART I
YOUR PORTFOLIO
AND ITS CONTENTS

From the Real World

B.J. Richardson is a middle school principal in a rural area of northern Illinois. He oversees 72 staff members and 580 sixth through eighth grade students. This is his second year as principal. With over 9 years of experience as an assistant principal and as a principal, B.J. has also served as District Testing Coordinator and Career Education Coordinator.

What makes me sit up and take notice?

- Enthusiasm, genuine care, and concern for student growth.
- Someone that can articulate a strong student centered mission.
- Someone that is polite, courteous, and on time for their appointment.
- Someone that can articulate their knowledge and ability to utilize Technology, State Standards, and an understanding of School Improvement Initiatives in their daily classroom instruction.
- Someone that consistently articulates a strong sense of self worth and team concept.
- Positive self image.
- Ability to ask questions that demonstrate a sincere interest in our school and in our district.
- Evidence of a sense of humor.

What sets off warning bells during an interview?

- Lack of any of the above.
- Poor communication skills.
- Appearance of saying what they think I want to hear.
- Trying to demonstrate, or "wing," knowledge or skills they do not possess.
- Untidy appearance.

Chapter 1: Teaching Portfolios: What are They, and Why Do You Need Them?

2

Chapter 1
Teaching Portfolios: What are They, and Why Do You Need Them?

"Educators of teachers have two essential ethical and legal responsibilities. One is to support the development of the teachers with whom they work. The other is fundamentally one of accountability and plays itself out in policy arrangements between the state and teacher education institutions (e.g., credential and accreditation). These two responsibilities of any teacher education program contain an inherent tension: How to provide supportive opportunities for learning while simultaneously being accountable to the standards set forth by the licensing agencies?" (Snyder, Lippincott, & Bower, 1998)

You can see the dilemma: educators wish to extract the personal best from the students, yet they must always look over their shoulders to see who is watching and evaluating them, the teachers. Enter: portfolios. Portfolios offer authentic assessment to both the educators and the administrators evaluating those educators. Some education majors claim that teaching portfolios are not worth the time they would have to invest in them. They may either feel confident that their skills will speak for themselves, or they sometimes believe that their achievements are not worth highlighting, and that it would be self-centered to focus so much attention on themselves. Either way, these educators are wrong. Maintaining portfolios of your skills and achievements is beneficial to you and to your future employers.

Why Portfolios?

A portfolio is more than a collection of your best teaching efforts; rather, a portfolio is a demonstration of your growth and improvement as a teacher (Farris, 1999). In this chapter, we'll explore three main reasons to maintain teaching portfolios:
- portfolios benefit you personally
- portfolios give your prospective employers valuable information about you
- portfolios help you to develop and voice your personal philosophies and theories of education.

How Portfolios Benefit You

As you complete your course credits, hours of study, and years of experience in college and in your pre-service student teaching endeavors, you are accumulating an on-going, vast array of outstanding examples of your growth as an educator. You will have papers of which you are particularly proud, glowing narrative descriptions of your first time in front of a group of students and critical but encouraging evaluations from your supervisors. Most importantly, you will have documentation that you possess both the desire and the knowledge necessary to become a dedicated professional and a life-long learner.

Chapter 1: Teaching Portfolios: What are They, and Why Do You Need Them?

3

Another personal reason to maintain portfolios is to keep records of those wonderful projects, bulletin boards, learning centers, and thematic units you've created. As the years fly by, the memories of those unique creations will fade and you'll find yourself wishing you had kept copies of them to adapt for future students. You may be an experienced educator who wishes to teach in a different area and could finally use all those projects you learned about and created, but never got the chance to pursue when you were an undergraduate. Or you may be taking post-graduate classes and would like to refer to all those wonderful activities you implemented when you student taught.

Finally, teaching portfolios provide times for reflection. Reflection is the ability and disposition to think deeply and make decisions about which strategy is appropriate at any given time (Arends, 1998). We educators often get so swept up in the day-to-day (or minute-to-minute) hectic world of teaching that we forget to stop and think about how our lessons have turned out, or how we feel about the day's events. Maintaining a portfolio gives you the opportunity to develop the healthy habit of reflecting on the success (or lack thereof) of a lesson. Saving student work that shows how you wanted the lesson to turn out validates you and reminds you why it worked. On the other hand, saving student work that shows how the lesson failed miserably provides valuable input as well. You can learn from your mistakes and chuckle ruefully as you come across the unfortunate samples years later. Either way, you are taking the time to consider the effects of your efforts—isn't that what we always wish for our students to do?[1]

How Portfolios Benefit Your Prospective Employers

Employers who are seeking new employees to join their staffs are in precarious positions. They must rely on subjective evaluations such as interviews, letters of recommendation from people who are strangers to them, and the word--possibly lip service--of those being interviewed. The opportunity to see, to have the time to read and reflect upon, a professional portfolio gives employers the chance to affirm or discredit their intuitions with hard facts. The professional portfolio eliminates doubt and reinforces the recommendations given by you and your personal references. While employers may not have the time or the opportunity to examine each and every portfolio that comes their way, they may have certain criteria in mind as they skim through the artifacts. Another way you can use the portfolio as you interview is to have it organized so neatly that you can immediately pull out a certain section as the topic arises in the interview. Consider color-coding artifacts or having a usable table of contents.

As you'll see in our personal notes from administrators, their position as the determiners of the fate of educators is not an enviable one. Employers must weed out the sincere from the false, the knowledgeable from the vague, and the actual best qualified from the best-worded applicants. Portfolios provide authentic assessment of an educator's skills, accomplishments, and teaching philosophy. Portfolios may include glowing letters of thanks from parents or students, awards from the school or community, and certificates of

---

[1] For more information on reflection, go to Chapter 2.

Chapter 1: Teaching Portfolios: What are They, and Why Do You Need Them?

4

additional coursework achieved. These artifacts compiled with complimentary letters of reference and moving personal statements all give employers a fair representation of exactly whom they're considering.

How Portfolios Help You Express Your Philosophy

Whether you realize it or not, you have already developed a philosophy or two regarding the field of education. There are instinctive answers to age-old questions regarding the purpose of schools and the best ways to teach, and the knowledgeable teacher realizes the importance of those philosophies. When you are aware of your points of view, you may speak more eloquently to issues of curriculum, classroom management, parental involvement, and the rights of both teachers and students. However, bear in mind that as you gain experiences in both your profession and in life in general, your philosophies of education may change.

As you apply for and interview for jobs, you will find that employers often ask either in person or on the applications for your philosophies of teaching. How do you plan to make a difference? Why do you wish to be a teacher? Having an answer ready for these questions shows that you are making an intentional decision to become an educator. Recognizing that your beliefs may change demonstrates your willingness to grow and to be a life-long learner.[2]

Types of Portfolios

The term "portfolio" is one of the most commonly-used buzz words in the education profession today. Some of the people most likely to use portfolios are undergraduate education majors, student teachers, new teachers, tenured teachers, and higher education faculty.

- Professional portfolios are maintained by undergraduate college students to document skills and experiences.
- Student teachers update their portfolios to prepare them for those crucial first interviews.
- New teachers keep all their lesson plans, evaluations, and communication documents in portfolios to show their organization, growth, and readiness for tenure.
- Tenured teachers wishing to become nationally certified, "master teachers" will include artifacts of post-graduate work accomplished, diversity of students taught, peer evaluations, letters of recommendation by parents and students, and copies of outstanding lesson plans and samples of student work following those plans.
- Finally, university level educators will wish to document their achievements, such as dissertations, publications, awards, speaking engagements, evaluations, and advanced coursework as they pursue full professorships.

As you can see, portfolio maintenance is developmental and on-going—one may even consider it to be a major component of being a professional educator.

---

[2] For more information on philosophies of education, see Chapter 3.

Chapter 1: Teaching Portfolios: What are They, and Why Do You Need Them?

5

The Professional Portfolio as a Concept

In their 1998 manual from the University of Maryland, *Developing a Professional Teaching Portfolio, A Guide for Educators* (1998) Constantino and DeLorenzo explore the development and use of portfolios. The importance of portfolios is outlined in the text with the below listed reasons. As you can see by these eight attributes, creating your own portfolio is clearly a worthwhile, necessary endeavor.

- Portfolios facilitate the development of reflective thinking.
- Portfolios present a holistic view of your achievements.
- Portfolios provide an ongoing record of your accomplishments.
- Portfolios place the responsibility on you to develop and plan for your goals.
- Portfolios correlate with national and state initiatives toward performance-based assessment.
- Portfolios may be used to document and validate teaching accomplishments.
- Portfolios may be used to assess preservice and inservice teacher performances.
- Portfolios enhance job searches and interview processes.

References

Arends, R. I., Winitzky, N. E., & Tannenbaum, M. D. (2001). *Exploring Teaching, Second Edition.* Boston: McGraw-Hill.

Constantino, P.M. & DeLorenzo, M.N. (1998). *Developing a Professional Teaching Portfolio, A Guide for Educators.* College Park, MD: University of Maryland.

Farris, P. J. (1999). *Teaching, Bearing the Torch, Second Edition.* Boston: McGraw-Hill.

Sadker, M., and Sadker, D. (2000). *Teachers, Schools, & Society, Fifth Edition.* Boston: McGraw-Hill.

Snyder, J., Lippincott, A., & Bower, D. (1998). The inherent tensions in the multiple uses of portfolios in teacher education. *Teacher Education Quarterly* 25 (1), 45-60.

Website Suggestions:

For an excellent example of a teaching portfolio created by veteran educator Martin Kimeldorf, visit his website. In addition to sharing his actual portfolio with you, Kimeldorf also explains why he feels it is important to use portfolios.

http://amby.com/kimeldorf/sampler/html

The American Association for Higher Education (AAHE) provides this guide to "Campus Use of the Teaching Portfolio: Twenty-Five Profiles."

http://www.bradley.edu/otefd/Library/Teacher-Portfolios.html

The list below has links to Web pages on Teaching Portfolios. The URLs are shown in square brackets, but you do not need these URLs if you click on the links.

http://www.cll.wayne.edu/fls/Teachptf.htm

Chapter 1: Teaching Portfolios: What are They, and Why Do You Need Them?

6

Notes

_____

_____

_____

_____

_____

_____

_____

_____

_____

_____

_____

_____

_____

_____

_____

_____

Chapter 1: Teaching Portfolios: What are They, and Why Do You Need Them?

7

From the Real World

--In Chapter One, B.J. Richardson shared with us his views on how to quickly interest or repel an interviewer. Now B.J. explains his interview process.

During interviews, I utilize the *Gallup Organizations Teacher Perceiver Interview*, for which I have received extensive and intensive training. The interview entails:
60 questions given to each candidate, which encompass these 12 teaching themes:

- Mission
- Empathy
- Rapport Drive
- Individualized Perception
- Listening
- Investment
- Input Drive
- Activation
- Innovation
- Gestalt
- Objectivity
- Focus

In addition to the 60 question Teacher Perceiver, I utilize questions that will key in on the individuals, their interests, and their understanding of Middle School students and Best Practices.

I also give each candidate one or both of the following questions, with a description of each:

- "If you could be any, which of these would you choose: Explorer, Pathfinder, Settler, or Stay-at-Homer?"
- "You've always wanted to be in the circus. It's in town and you can be one of the following: Ring Master, Clown, Lion Tamer, or Juggler. Which do you choose, and why?"
- Finally, I always ask if they were the successful candidate, how long would it take them to make their decision.

Chapter 2
What Goes in a Teaching Portfolio?

Many renowned experts in the field of education have researched the uses of portfolios and made recommendations for design. In the fifth edition of *Teachers, Schools, & Society* (Sadker & Sadker, McGraw-Hill 2000) Phyllis Learner describes your portfolio as a tool that is:

- Purposeful
- Selective
- Diverse
- Ongoing
- Reflective
- Collaborative

Purposeful and Selective: This portfolio will show your intentional, thoughtful alertness to detail in the items included. Each section will have a specific purpose. Learner recommends basing your portfolio upon a set of national standards. Another possibility is to research the school districts you're applying to and make the portfolio specific to their priorities. For example, if they are currently advocating full inclusion in their classrooms, your portfolio will reflect your ability to team teach, to work with parents, to utilize support staff effectively, and to appropriately modify your curriculum and instruction.

Diverse and Ongoing: Remember that your professors and administrators are interested in more than a one-dimensional documentation of courses taken and clinicals you've experienced. Any experiences with children and with the community are relevant to your abilities and your willingness to go the extra mile for students and for your educational community. Keep your portfolio diverse by including items displaying your involvement with your church, university organizations, or community. Make the presentation engaging with a variety of mediums used: photos, news articles, letters of thanks, certificates of achievement, and other worthy entries.

Ongoing refers to the need to keep your portfolio current. Regardless of your level of experience, as an educator you will always be learning and growing. Your portfolio should display this growth. However, remember to be intentional: use the artifacts that best represent your abilities, interests, and commitment without causing your portfolio to seem cluttered or inefficient.

Reflective and collaborative: We've already addressed the importance of reflection in portfolios, and you will encounter the topic again in this text. *Collaborative* is a term with several positive meanings. One definition of being collaborative indicates that you are a team player, willing to work with your colleagues, fellow staff members, parents, community, and students to provide the best possible education to your students. Another definition of collaborative addresses the need to display the role others played in your portfolio. You may have team-taught a lesson in class or completed a group project. Perhaps you and your professor maintained a dialogue journal during your clinical experiences. A third possiblility for collaboration is asking others to provide feedback on your portfolio. It is important to determine whether your portfolio reflects your intended message to its audience.

The following outline provides a general guide to the categories and items suggested for inclusion in a teaching portfolio. It is important to bear in mind that your portfolio must reflect your personality more than your ability to follow a how-to portfolio "recipe."

SUGGESTED TABLE OF CONTENTS FOR A TEACHING PORTFOLIO

A.   Statement of Teaching Philosophy[1]

B.   Credentials
   1. letters of reference
   2. resume
   3. official transcript
   4. record of courses
   5. teaching certificate
   6. endorsements

C.   Teaching-related Experiences
   1. Pre-professional clinical experiences
   2. Employment in child-related fields
   3. Volunteer work with children
   4. Student teaching experiences
      a. sample lesson plans
      b. reflective journal
      c. sample student work
      d. photos of bulletin boards or projects you created
      e. letters from students or parents
      f. evaluations by university supervisor
      g. evaluations by cooperating/mentor teacher
   5. Classroom management plan
      a. sample discipline referral form
      b. sample letters to parents
      c. sample team policy
   6. Curricular Modifications
   7. How your lesson plans reflect state or national goals[2]

D.   Community Involvement
   1. Descriptions of volunteerism (other than earlier mentioned child-related)
   2. Copies of articles concerning or actual certificates of local awards or scholarships won
   3. Photos or articles concerning church or civic group participation

E.   Professional Memberships & Honor Societies
   1. Certificates of membership in student chapters of professional groups, such as Council for Exceptional Children, International Reading Association, National Council for Teachers of Mathematics, National Education Association, etc.
   2. Certificates of membership or articles concerning membership in academic or service-related honor societies such as Phi Delta Kappa, Mortar Board, Omicron Delta Kappa, etc.

F.   Extracurricular Activities
   1. Experience with sports you would be able to coach
   2. Experiences with journalism, yearbook, or other media
   3. Experiences with other club activities, such as chess, international clubs, or career-related clubs
   4. Roles of leadership in the above organizations

---

[1] For more information on how to state your educational philosophy, see Chapter 6.

[2] For more information on national standards, see Chapter 4.

The next artifacts are examples of a Record of Courses and a resume of a beginning teacher. If you are writing a resume and have not yet obtained a degree or teacher certification, you can state your anticipated date of graduation and the certificates you will be applying and testing for. Also stress the importance of your other areas of employment that involved working with children or roles of leadership.

Joseph E. Pourroy
1313 Mockingbird Lane
Anytown, Illinois 12345
(123)456-7890

Career Objective:
To instill a love of learning in my students that will enable them to develop their talents and interests so they can become productive citizens of the world.

Education:
Bachelor of Science in Education, Northern Illinois University (May, 1998)
Major: Elementary Education
Certification: Type 03, with a Middle School endorsement

Teaching Experience:
Alternative Education Instructor, Kishwaukee Education Consortium
August, 1998 to June, 1999.
Student Teacher, 2nd Grade, DeKalb School District #428
January, 1998 - May, 1998.
Outdoor Education Facilitator, 3rd Grade, Laredo Taft Campus, Northern Illinois University
February, 1998.
Junior Block Practicum, 2nd Grade, Carpentersville District 300
October, 1997 - November, 1997.
Volunteer Instructor, Gross Motor Development Lab, Northern Illinois University
June, 1997 - August, 1997.
Sophomore Block Practicum, 7th Grade, West Chicago Unified School District
Spring, 1997.

Employment History:
August, 1998 – Present.
Kishwaukee Education Consortium, **Alternative Education Instructor**

December, 1997 - Present.
Gurler Heritage Association, **Caretaker:** Gurler House
Live in historic home/community center. Provide security, tours, and light maintenance of house and grounds, participate in community events, help to coordinate September 20-26, 1998 Gurler House Week with DeKalb Schools.

June, 1996 - March, 1998; Summer, 1998.
Northern Illinois University, **Desk Clerk:** College of Law Library
Monitor front desk, filed legal journal updates and materials.

1979 - 1995
Duplex Products Inc., **Printing Press Operator:** Responsible for set up and operation of four-color wet offset web press.

1980 - 1994
United States Soccer Federation, **Referee:** Northern Illinois Soccer League, U-14 and under.
Joseph Pourroy, page 2

Church Leadership
1993 - Present.
Unitarian Universalist Fellowship of DeKalb. Past and present positions include CROP Walk Coordinator, Newsletter Editor, Board President, and Religious Education teacher.

Memberships Professional:
International Reading Association
Association for Supervision and Curriculum Development

Community Service:
Fall, 1995
DeKalb Public Schools Mentoring Program, Mentored 5th grade boy.

1993 - Present.
DeKalb Area Women's Center, Volunteer and member.

August, 1993 – Present.
Interfaith Network for Peace and Justice, Steering Committee Member and Annual Garage Sale Co-Coordinator

August, 1992 – Present.
DeKalb CornFest, Art Fest Volunteer Instructor

1980 - 1995
American Youth Soccer Organization, Referee, evaluator, and trainer

Implications

First impressions are permanent and can make or break your opportunity with a district. It is important to research the school districts you're interested in before you organize your portfolio for interviews. Regardless of the type of district you choose to apply to, documents that will be appropriate for inclusion are a Table of Contents to make your portfolio simple to use, a Record of Courses to display the courses you've completed successfully, and a resume focusing on your experiences with children in and out of the classroom.

References

Sadker, M., and Sadker, D. (2000). *Teachers, Schools, & Society, Fifth Edition.* Boston: McGraw-Hill.

Website Suggestions:

For more information on writing resumes and other employment tips, go to

http://www.virtualresume.com/

Another engaging site is the "Damn Good Resume" website. For suggested readings, examples of resumes, weblinks, and other relevant information, go to

http://www.damngood.com/

For examples of resumes, writing tips, and related links, go to

http://www.4resumes.com/

Notes

_____

_____

_____

_____

_____

_____

_____

_____

_____

_____

_____

_____

_____

_____

_____

_____

_____

_____

From the Real World

--Michael Devereaux, Elementary School Principal

My name is Michael Devereaux. I've been in education for 26 years, 21 as an elementary principal. Our school is Walnut Hills Elementary, Greenville, MI. It is a small urban area about 35 miles NW of Grand Rapids, MI. Our school population is 350+ students. We have about 50 professionals and paraprofessionals working in our school throughout each week. During my 26 years I've been involved with over 100 interviews of paraprofessionals, teachers, and administrators at the building level and central office level.

I have found that a teaching portfolio is an excellent tool to give an enhanced "picture" of the teaching candidate. However, in my opinion, the portfolio must be meaningful, not cluttered, somewhat colorful and attractive, and above all organized (table of contents; body; and appendices). The portfolio must enhance the candidate: awards; certifications; transcripts; letters of reference; correct spelling/grammar; and of course working with children.

What will make me notice a candidate is the first impression: better than proper attire; smile; composure; professional language/diction; and a sense of humor. What will be "red flags" are the opposites of the above. The misspelling of words in an application, portfolio, or communication is an obvious "red flag." One thing I focus on while reading an application is the Reference Section. I will look to see if I know any listed reference. My advice is to personalize your references, by that I mean, DO put down those references who will help enhance your "picture." Think of any reference that may be connected to the school where you are applying. Think of any reference who lives in the area of the school where you are applying—personalize your references.

Chapter 3
Styles of Portfolios

In addition to your appearance, attitude, and responses to questions, your portfolio is an extremely important portrayal of your skills, knowledge, and values. Mr. Devereaux demonstrates this in his insightful comments. What style of portfolio best calls attention to your strengths, your personality?

There are many style options to consider when designing your portfolio. From the type of stationery and font used to the artifacts you choose to include, there are myriad decisions to be made. As previously mentioned, it is important to keep in mind the purpose of your portfolio as you create it. If you are creating a portfolio for assessment in a course, naturally you will follow the instructor's guidelines. When preparing a portfolio to take on an interview, you should set up your portfolio to show that you have researched the school district. Portfolios for certifications will have another set of standards to meet.

Along with presenting hard copies of your portfolio, there are alternate ways to display portfolios. Portfolios may be presented in web pages online; however, bear in mind that not all administrators have the luxury or the training to be able to access the Internet from their offices. Another method of presentation is the Digital Portfolio.

Digital Portfolios
One advancement in the field of portfolio development is the innovative Digital Portfolio. A digital, or electronic, portfolio is "…a purposeful collection of work, captured by electronic means, that serves as an exhibit of individual efforts, progress, and achievements in one or more areas." (Wiedmer, 1998.) Digital portfolios may be given on disk or on CD-rom, or may be sent by email as attachments. Unlike hard copies, digital portfolios may be interactive with the use of Power Point, hyperlinks, sound, and video.

According to Wiedmer, digital portfolios reflect the depth of involvement of the individual in both selection and design. Additionally, digital portfolios with their ability to transmit vivid images with sight and sound can more accurately capture and transmit in attention-getting ways the personality of the candidate.

Another benefit of digital portfolios that should not be overlooked is almost obvious: if a presenter is using computers to generate a portfolio, then that presenter's aptitude for technological advancement must be current and also improving as new innovations in technology arrive. (Georgi & Crowe, 1998.)

Issues regarding the creation of effective electronic portfolios address what the candidate should know and be able to do; how the individual can demonstrate his/her vision; what types of reliable hardware and software are needed; how to select and use artifacts; and what culture, or audience, will be receiving the portfolio. (Wiedmer, 1998.)

Digital portfolios may include, but are not limited to, the following types of artifacts:

- Website of applicant including resume, letters of reference, statement of philosophy
- Video clip of applicant teaching a lesson
- Links to other websites where the applicant can be found, such as the sites of other organizations, or newspapers that have articles about the applicant
- Power point presentation of the applicant's strengths and how they will benefit the school district
- List of applicant's technological abilities, with links to examples of each
- Applicant's teaching certificates, test scores, and other documents can be scanned into the website

Aesthetic Style

The use of the term aesthetics in this chapter simply refers to the attractiveness, or the pleasure factor, of your portfolio. Always keep the audience in mind as you design your portfolio. Keep the layout attractive and colorful, without appearing too busy, or crowded. Consider the captions to use with your photographs. Survey your friends to determine which fonts and font sizes on your word processor are the easiest to read. Avoid extreme colors that may cause the audience to squint—you want to catch their eyes, not give them headaches.

Use an easy-to-follow format, which guides the reader through your portfolio in a comfortable manner. It is recommended that you have a table of contents[1], paginate your artifacts, have labeled sections, and also consider using color-coded tabs as guides. In addition to increasing your audience's incentive to read through your artifacts, this type of organization will also help you when you wish to refer to a specific item during an interview. There are pros and cons to consider when deciding whether or not to use clear plastic page protectors. The reasons to use them are they are neat, they keep pages from being crumpled, and they eliminate the need to hole-punch important documents. One reason to avoid using them is they are cumbersome, taking up much more weight and space than do single pages.

If you include photos, certificates, or other oddly-shaped items, you may wish to use a scanner instead of including the actual documents. Using a scanner will allow you to keep your precious documents at home and give you space to write explanations of the importance of the documents beneath their scanned photos.

Efferent Style

The term efferent describes information giving and receiving. In terms of efference, consider exactly what information you wish to convey to your audience. Which artifacts will need explaining, which are self-explanatory? Will you point out the highlights of lengthy, detailed documents such as your Record of Courses, (which is addressed in the chapter on professional growth)? Which references will best display your work ethics,

---

[1] See Chapter 2 for ideas on what to include in the table of contents.

child-related skills, and sense of purpose? Will you section your portfolio according to a certain set of teaching standards, or would you rather name your sections in a more personal, self-evaluative manner? As you view your portfolio, ask yourself what items command attention, are memorable. Ask a friend to critically read your portfolio, then tell you exactly what the portfolio communicates about you. Also consider asking an acquaintance that does not know you as well to do the same. If the qualities you wish to convey are not evident according to your reviewers, what can you do to make those qualities stand out?

Borko, et al (1997) identified and discussed several purposes for creating portfolios. Which of these purposes is evident in your portfolio?

- For evaluation and to secure employment
- To be graded, such as in a professional seminar
- To represent you as a teacher, i.e.: your teaching philosophy and style
- To provide a stimulus for reflection on your teaching and to develop your identity
- To be a vehicle for advancing your professional development.

Sample Artifacts

The following pages demonstrate a few of the types of items appropriate for inclusion. After you've looked over these items, take time to brainstorm on your notes page a list of items you would like to include in your portfolio.

Our first artifact, Tanya's reflection, includes a colorful, attractive photo of the bulletin board she created. In addition to showing her creativity, Tanya is also demonstrating how she incorporated the school's ideals into her display.

SAMPLE ARTIFACT
Clinical Experience
Fall, 1999
Tanya Gorham

…There was much diversity in the class with students ranging in a wide variety of reading levels. Since I did not attend every day, the observation was very choppy. (The teacher) used a literacy framework when teaching the students. The students were broken up into groups with different reading levels, from third to fifth grade reading abilities. Each day the groups would read articles ranging in difficulty. Not every group would meet every day, but it was divided up among the week. Her reading and teaching in general also followed the material framework guidelines. She often used published school reading programs. The articles the students read in the groups were chosen with questions listed to ask about each article. The reason I say she incorporated a literacy framework also is the fact that she did not simply teach from the direct basal of the third grade level, but she expanded it to meet the various levels of her students. Of the nine major components of reading comprehension and response, she incorporated several that I observed. She used social aspects. The school was big on making connections when reading. That was what my bulletin picture was based upon. The students were to make text to self, text to text, and text to work connections while reading. They could use post-it notes to keep track of these. Then, together as a class, they would discuss their findings and add them to a poster.

In this artifact, Joe presents his invention: Spelling Word Baseball. By including this spelling baseball game, Joe demonstrates his ability to create engaging methods to reinforce his students' spelling skills. This artifact should be included in his lesson plan component.

SAMPLE ARTIFACT
Joe Pourroy

Spelling Word Baseball

Prepare for game day by marking index cards as follows and placing them in a container.
- Single (4 cards)
- Double (2 cards)
- Triple (1 card)
- Home Run (1 card)
- Out (3 cards)

Also have prepared slips of paper with spelling words printed on them.

On the day of the game solicit the help of an artist in the class to draw a baseball diamond on the board. Divide the class into two teams. To begin, a player from the team "at bat" draws a file card and the pitching team draws a word slip to "pitch" to the designated speller. If the player at bat draws a single, he/she must spell the word correctly to get a person to first base. For a double, he/she must spell the word correctly *and* provide a definition of the word. A triple requires that he/she spell the word correctly, provide a definition, *and* use the word in a sentence. Finally, to earn a home run the player must spell the word correctly, provide a definition, use the word in a sentence, *and* break the word into syllables.

Pick one team to bat first and after the batting team decides upon their batting line up, each player goes in order until the batting team gets three outs. Outs are counted when the team either draws an "out" card or fails to correctly spell the word. Any correct spelling gets them safely on base and no penalty is incurred if they fail to define the word, use it in a sentence, or break it into syllables.

Neither set of cards should be returned to the container until a side has "struck out." The game is over when a pre-specified number of innings (depending upon the amount of time available) have been played.

Following Joe's artifact in the portfolio, it would be appropriate to also include a rationale and reflection, such as:

I am including this spelling activity because it shows my ability to create fun, relevant reinforcing activities that will appeal to a variety of learning styles, preferences, and abilities. Students who are uncomfortable spelling will enjoy the appeal of also being allowed to "pitch" words to their peers and may learn more spelling words while listening. Students adept at spelling are often bored with routine spelling lessons and will enjoy the unusual way to demonstrate their knowledge. Kinetic learners will benefit from being allowed to be out of their seats and moving around the bases. Students with English as a second language may have very little knowledge of baseball and will be both learning baseball terms and practicing their spelling and vocabulary skills.

In addition to meeting many different learning needs, this activity also meets State Language Arts Goal #3A, "Students will use correct grammar, spelling, punctuation, capitalization, and structure."

If I had my own classroom, I would consider designing an integrated unit on baseball. We could decorate the room as a baseball stadium in art, learn about baseball statistics in math, study the cities having professional baseball teams in social studies, watch classic movies about baseball heroes in homeroom, and write research reports about topics related to baseball in language arts.

Tiffany, a freshman in the College of Education, has not yet had any clinical experiences to include in her portfolio. What she is able to include, however, is this moving description of her involvement in an evening recreational program for inner-city children.

SAMPLE ARTIFACT
Tiffany Banks
Fall, 1999

KIDS' NIGHT

When I worked at McDonald's I was assigned to be in charge of "Kids' Night." This program was every Tuesday. Children could get kids meals for a dollar. I was the one who organized activities for the kids to participate in. I soon discovered there was one group of kids that always came. They always appeared to be excited to spend time with me. That made me feel very special.

As time went by, I started to care for the kids a lot. It concerned me that their parents were not around a lot. Did they know where they were? I met each parent once, out of a five-month period. Most of them were happy about the program, mainly because they considered it a free babysitting service. It was clear to see that most of these parents were drug addicts or prostitutes. Some of the parents were also violent. At least five of the children had been abused. I could see the fear the kids had when their parents were around, they could hardly look at them. The intimidations between the kids and their parents were strong.

The thing that I admired most about the kids was that through all the pain, they could still show love. They really respected me and cared a lot about me. It's funny because I had to quit my job due to conflicts with my boss. I explained that to them (the kids). So they all gathered together and told my boss off. I was so proud of them, although it was wrong.

I think about them a lot and wonder how they are. I was mad because when I left, the activities were canceled because nobody wanted to take over the job. This meant the kids had nowhere to go.

"Kids' Night" shows the reader Tiffany's respect and love for the inner-city children that came to her program, and demonstrates her willingness to help disadvantaged, abused, and neglected children to overcome formidable obstacles.

Implications

Student teachers and veteran teachers alike may wish to consider using digital portfolios to electronically, effectively communicate their talents, skills, and personalities. Criteria established for evaluating portfolios indicate that portfolios should reflect components of purpose, selectivity, diversity, ongoing/developmental, reflection, and collaboration.

When designing your portfolio, you should consider both aesthetic and efferent purposes. Aesthetics relate to the emotions or pleasure experienced when reading a portfolio; efference refers to the information obtained and relayed in a portfolio. It is wise to have others read through your portfolio and share with you the messages your portfolio conveys to them.

Portfolios may be designed to earn grades, to help you to reflect and grow, to advance professional development, to demonstrate your teaching philosophy and style, and to share with potential employers.

References

Borko, H., et al (1997). Student teaching portfolios: A tool for promoting reflective practice. *Journal of Teacher Education* 48 (5), 345-357.

Georgi, D. & Crowe, J. (1998). Digital portfolios: A confluence of portfolio assessment and technology. *Teacher Education Quarterly* 25 (1), 73-84.

Wiedmer, T.L. (1998). Digital portfolios: Capturing and demonstrating skills and levels of performance. *Phi Delta Kappan* 79 (8), 586-589.

Website Suggestions:

This website describes a CD-ROM that guides you on the design and content issues on making effective Web portfolios.
http://zeus.ia.net/~achrazog/index.html

This page provides links (without comment) to a variety of teaching portfolios online.
http://www.utep.edu/cetal/portfoli/samples.html

This website from the Los Angeles County Office of Education guides the viewer through the main tenets and helpful hints for student portfolios, teacher portfolios, and electronic portfolios.
http://www.lacoe.edu/pdc/second/portfolio.html

This website by Zella M. Boulware, Ed.D. and Dennis M. Holt, Ph.D. of the University of North Florida College of Education and Human Services, Division of Curriculum and Instruction explains to preservice teachers how to use CD-ROM technology to develop portfolios.
http://www.unf.edu/faculty/dholt/using.html

NOTES

_____

_____

_____

_____

_____

_____

_____

_____

_____

_____

_____

_____

_____

_____

_____

_____

_____

_____

_____

From the Real World

--B.J. Richardson

Last from B.J. Richardson, words of advice…

What to never, ever, do or say when being interviewed:

- Don't get hung up on the salary schedule or benefits. Do ask about these in a Professional Growth context.
- Don't be overly aggressive or argumentative.
- Don't dress in a provocative manner.
- *If you are using a portfolio, make sure it contains only those items you wish to accentuate and will utilize. Skipping and skimming are "no-no's." Also be sure you have practiced your delivery of your portfolio with friends or relatives.*
- Never use references that cast you in a bad light (you laugh, but his has happened!)
- Don't come across as a "yes" person.
- Never beg or articulate how "badly" you need this position.
- Never use "yeah," "nah," "whatever," or other slang terms.
- Refrain from the use of profanity.
- Never ask or key in on questions about the required length of the teachers' day.

And more positive advice, B.J.?

- Be honest and open.
- Do not hesitate to ask questions about the school and its use of technology, **_State Standards_**, School Improvement, etc.
- Be sure to inquire about extra curricular areas you would like to participate in.
- Don't be afraid to ask about the mentoring program.
- Try to be calm and objective. Remember, you are interviewing the school as much as they are interviewing you. Be sure you are comfortable with the things you hear and see.
- Before the interview, ask for information, such as the School Report Card or the Curricular Guide. Reference this information during your discussion, but make sure the reference fits the current topic.
- BE YOURSELF.

Chapter 4
Using Standards to Construct Your Portfolio

Notice that B.J. Richardson included state standards in his list of questions to ask. It is extremely important for you to be well-versed in the standards of the districts you apply to. In your college prep courses, your instructors will emphasize their own state's standards; however, if you wish to teach in a different state, you will need to research their standards, as well.[1]

As you design your portfolio, it may help you to structure it according to a specified set of standards.[2] This chapter delineates several national standards programs and also provides information on standards for specialized fields.

I.   **INTASC**
       The Interstate New Teacher Assessment and Support Consortium (INTASC) has identified ten standards for what beginning teachers should know. Briefly, these components include:
       1.   Knowledge of subject
       2.   Learning and human development
       3.   Adapting instruction
       4.   Strategies
       5.   Motivation and classroom management
       6.   Communication skills
       7.   Planning
       8.   Assessment
       9.   Commitment
       10.   Partnerships
       (Martin, 1999)

It is noteworthy to add that the National Council for Accreditation of Teacher Education (NCATE) uses the INTASC standards to evaluate teacher education programs. For a fine example of how to apply lessons to INTASC standards, read the fifth edition of *Teachers, Schools, and Society* (Sadker, 2000.) Another way to organize your portfolio according to INTASC is presented in the following section.

Organizing Your Portfolio in Relation to Standards
It may help you and your prospective employers if you arrange your portfolio according to a set of standards adopted by their school, district, or state. One modification to the following table of contents that you may wish to consider is to cross-reference the artifacts that address

---

[1] See Appendix B for State Departments of Education and Certification.
[2] See Appendix A for addresses and websites of many professional organizations.

more than one standard. For example, lesson plans would be appropriate to include in several areas such as learning and human development, adapting instruction, motivation and classroom management, and planning. Another example is your participation in community events that benefit children, which may fit under the commitment, partnership, and communication standards.

This table of contents is based upon the INTASC standards; however when you organize your portfolio be sure to determine which standards are most often used in your region.

SUGGESTED TABLE OF CONTENTS BASED ON INTASC

I. **Standard: Knowledge of Subject**
    A. Record of Courses
    B. Practicum/Clinical experience
    C. Research papers
    D. Certificates of completion of workshops
    E. Summaries of related articles
    F. Bibliography of related texts

II. **Standard: Learning and Human Development**
    A. Sample lesson plans created for a variety of age groups
    B. Reflections on the difference between your 2nd grade clinical students and your 6th grade clinical students
    C. A bibliography of children's books with suggestions for age-appropriateness
    D. Term paper comparing and contrasting the theories of renowned child psychologists

III. **Standard: Adapting Instruction**
    A. Group project completed in your mainstreaming class
    B. Descriptions of curricular modifications you've tried and their outcomes
    C. Reflection on the role you played in an IEP meeting
    D. Letter from parents thanking you for the extra time you put into modifying the social studies test for their child with learning disabilities
    E. Examples of how you make curriculum more challenging for students with gifted abilities
    F. Narrative paper on your decision-making process when creating lesson plans to include students with English as a second language

IV. **Standard: Strategies**
    A. Video of you teaching a lesson
    B. Self-evaluation identifying methods you've found success with and others that still need work
    C. Narrative descriptions of the methods used by your cooperating teachers
    D. Research project on the battles of controversy between experts in the field of classroom instruction
    E. Rationale for changing cooperative learning groups before mid-semester

V. **Standard: Motivation and Classroom Management**
    A. Letters home updating parents on coming projects and homework
    B. Examples of certificates you've created for achievements such as:
        1. improved behavior
        2. excellent effort
        3. all homework in on time for the month
        4. improved attendance
    C. Copy of classroom assertive discipline plan, including:
        1. rules
        2. consequences
        3. student/teacher-generated reward system
        4. charts
    D. Certificate of completion of special classroom management course, seminar, or workshop
    E. Letters of appreciation from parents grateful for the extra effort you gave to their child with emotional or behavioral problems
    F. Summaries of articles on classroom management and/or motivation

VI. **Standard: Communication Skills**
  A. Letter to parents introducing yourself as student teacher
  B. Copies of minutes from team meetings showing your participation
  C. Copies of position or persuasive papers you've written
  D. Copies of group projects you've completed, demonstrating your ability to work in a group
  E. Certificates of your technological abilities, including:
    1. word processing
    2. internet
    3. data base
    4. spread sheets
    5. hyper links
    6. digital cameras
    7. scanners
  F. Address of your website with hard copies of documents included there
  G. Samples of your best handwriting in a hand-written essay (many districts require this in their employment applications)
  H. A video of you presenting a lesson to a class
  I. Powerpoint presentation of your philosophy of teaching

VII. **Standard: Planning**
  A. Copies of lesson plans from each subject and grade level you've worked with
  B. Copies of curriculum you've created
  C. Copies of group presentations you've team-taught in your courses
  D. A schedule of the entire schoolday from your clinical experience
  E. Examples of seating charts you've designed
  F. Scope and sequence of a unit you wish to teach

VIII. **Standard: Assessment**
  A. Copies of established informal assessment charts you've used, citing authors
  B. Copies of informal assessments you've created, including your rationale
  C. Copies of objective tests you've created
  D. Examples of how you modify assessments for students with special learning needs
  E. Skill inventories you've used or would like to use
  F. Learning modality inventories you've learned how to use
  G. Summaries of articles on multiple intelligences
  H. Papers you've written on multicultural issues in assessment

IX. **Standard: Commitment**
  A. Your statement of beliefs/philosophy of education
  B. Certificates of participation in community events
  C. Articles about your volunteer work with non-profit groups
  D. Your resume, focusing on the time you've spent working with children in and out of the school setting

X. **Standard: Partnerships**
  A. Documentation of the help you provided to coordinate a community volunteer drive for your local public school system
  B. Your written thoughts on a legislative session you attended in your state's capital when they discussed education issues
  C. Letters from your local legislators thanking you for meeting with them to discuss education issues

D.	Minutes from the school board meeting you attended to observe how their decision-making process works

E.	Letters from a parent/teacher organization thanking you for your help

F.	Letters you've written to local businesses suggesting ways that they can participate to help improve public education in your town

NBPTS

Another national standards organization is the National Board for Professional Teaching Standards (NBPTS). Created by the Carnegie Forum in the 1990's to recognize outstanding educators, the NBPTS identifies five core propositions, then also breaks these propositions down into standards and goals for each individual discipline. The five propositions are:

1.	Teachers are committed to students and their learning.
2.	Teachers know the subjects they teach and how to teach those subjects to students.
3.	Teachers are responsible for managing and monitoring student learning.
4.	Teachers think systematically about their practice and learn from experience.
5.	Teachers are members of learning communities.
	(NBPTS, 1999)

The NBPTS also has available several ancillaries such as a handbook and detailed guidelines for various disciplines.

Specialized Standards

Many educational associations have generated their own standards for their specific areas of interest. These organizations may be based upon subject, grade level, ability level, gender, race, or culture of students. Organizations such as those listed below offer guidelines, networks, standards, curriculum, and many more valuable resources. If you are applying for a specialized position, you may wish to organize your portfolio according to the standards of your special field.

NAEYC

A more age-specific national organization is the National Association for the Education of Young Children (NAEYC). The NAEYC has identified five major principles for its educators:

1.	Creating a caring community
2.	Teaching to enhance development and learning
3.	Constructing appropriate curriculum
4.	Assessing children's learning and development
5.	Establishing reciprocal relationships with families

NCTE and IRA

The National Council for Teachers of English (NCTE) and the International Reading Association (IRA) have collaborated to create standards for language arts. Their "Standards for Teaching Reading and Writing for Grades K through 12," recommend that rather than experiencing reading and writing in isolation and in small periods of time, students should be engaged in activities that emphasize the interaction of reading and writing for large blocks of time (e.g., lasting 3-5 days.) (Maxwell, 1997)

The twelve IRA/NCTE Standards for the English Language Arts are briefly summarized here; for a comprehensive list, order a copy from the National Council of Teachers of English, 1111 W. Kenyon Rd., Urbana, Illinois 61801-1096, or from the International Reading Association, 800 Barksdale Rd., P.O. Box 8139, Newark, Delaware 19714-8139.

1. Students read a wide range of print and nonprint texts to build an understanding … to acquire new information…Among these texts are fiction and nonfiction, classic and contemporary works.
2. Students read a wide range of literature from many periods in many genres...
3. Students apply a wide range of strategies to comprehend, interpret, evaluate, and appreciate texts…
4. Students adjust their use of all forms of language to communicate effectively.
5. Students employ a wide range of strategies to communicate with different audiences for a variety of purposes.
6. Students apply knowledge…to create, critique, and discuss print and nonprint texts.
7. Students conduct research…gather, evaluate, and synthesize data…
8. Students use a variety of technological and informational resources…
9. Students develop understanding and respect for diversity…
10. Students whose first language is not English use their first language to develop competency in the English language arts…
11. Students participate as knowledgeable, reflective…members of a variety of literacy communities.
12. Students use (various modes of) language to accomplish their own purposes.
(IRA/NCTE, 1996)

Implications

One reason to maintain a portfolio is to demonstrate that your knowledge of issues such as goals and standards is current. By organizing your portfolio according to a set of standards, you will convey your interest in helping your school district and your students to meet standards, and will also show your involvement with educational organizations.

References

Martin, D.B. (1999). The Portfolio Planner: Making Professional Portfolios Work For You. Upper Saddle River, NJ: Merrill.

Maxwell, M. (1997). Improving Student Learning Skills, A New Editon. Clearwater, FL: H & H Publishing Company, Inc.

National Board for Professional Teaching Standards (1999.) What Teachers Should Know and Be Able To Do. Southfield, MI: NBPTS.

National Council of Teachers of English and International Reading Association (1996). *Standards for the English Language Arts*. Urbana, IL: NCTE.

Sadker, M., and Sadker, D. (2000). *Teachers, Schools, & Society, Fifth Edition*. Boston: McGraw-Hill.

Website Suggestions:

For details and descriptions of the INTASC standards, go to
http://www.ccsso.org/intaspub.html

For more information on NAEYC's standards, go to
www.naeyc.org

For more information or to request a copy of the standards for your specific disciplines, call 1-800-22-TEACH, or go to the National Board for Professional Teaching Standards website at
www.nbpts.org

For more information on NCATE go to
http://ncate.org/

For more information on integrated reading and writing standards, go to
http://www.ncte.org/ or http://www.ira.org/

NOTES

_____

_____

_____

_____

_____

_____

_____

_____

_____

_____

_____

_____

_____

_____

_____

_____

PART II
PRESENTING YOUR
PROFESSIONAL BEST

SAMPLE ARTIFACT

Liz Newby
Clinical Reflection
Fall, 1999

...From working with Mrs. C., I definitely want to try a word wall. I found this to be extremely helpful to the children for learning "high frequency" words that the students would find in the books and poems they read. The word wall served as a basis for the words Mrs. C. expected them to read, and eventually, to spell. She also had the students have a "toughies box" at their desks. These were words that were giving them trouble and that they needed extra practice with. Whenever there was down time she would have the students work on these or read a book from their book boxes. I also will always remember how well Mrs. C. was organized. That is something that is important to me. She was also very good at explaining the day's activities to the children so that they knew what was going to happen during the day. She always tried to involve them in the decision-making process. She definitely used a literacy framework. She was always finding what worked best with her students.

Chapter 5
The Need For Reflection

"Reflection in teaching is a process that takes place over long periods of time in which connections, long strands of connections, are made between one's values, purposes, and actions towards engaging students successfully in their own meaningful language." (Lyons, 1998)

Good teachers are insightful. They combine their desire to share their knowledge with their daunting goal of meeting the individual needs of each student. One great contributor to the development of insight is the practice of reflection, or reflective teaching. In your portfolio, reflective artifacts will demonstrate to your future employers, peer review teams, or national standard review boards that you make intentional decisions. You are a teacher who monitors and adjusts your instruction to meet the needs of your students. Because you regularly reflect upon your lessons, your communication skills, and your curricular knowledge, you are obviously one whose goal is to use your ongoing, life-long learning to benefit your students, your school, and even your community at large.

Goals of Reflection

Reflective thinking is a means to enhance self-awareness, create a positive (albeit sometimes uncomfortable) lack of complacency, and keep oneself focused on improving professional practices. Also known as reflective teaching, reflective thinking exercises are tools for growth. When you practice reflection, you may be surprised to note that you are achieving several goals at the same time.

- One goal of reflection is self-evaluation. Ask yourself, "How do I feel about how my lesson turned out today?" Or ask, "Am I happy with myself as a teacher? If so, what growth am I observing? What new successes? If I'm dissatisfied, what specific areas can I improve? What is in my control, and what is not?"
- Another goal of reflection considers your impact on your students. When considering your students, focus on questions of comprehension, learning climate, frustration levels, and mastery of skills. "Whom did I observe showing mastery of the concept? Who was unusually quiet? Why did Billy act out today during the lesson, when he has not been a problem before? How can I get more students to volunteer answers? What's the best way to get Mary to try some problems on her own before she asks for help?"
- A third goal of reflective thinking is to make connections. These connections may relate to ideas of instruction, commonalties across curriculum, inspirations for interdisciplinary units, or even connections between causes and effects that occur in your classroom environment or between you and your colleagues, you and your students, or you and your students' parents.
- Finally, reflection is involved in your decisions regarding the artifacts that you include in your professional portfolio. Later in this chapter we'll explore several questions to reflect upon as you develop your portfolio.

Models of Reflection

From your first pre-professional experience to your application for a national master teaching certificate, you will have many reasons to reflect. The best way to keep records of your reflections is to maintain a reflection journal. In your journal, you may wish to follow Schon's (1987) guidelines for reflection. Schon suggests that there are two major types of reflective thinking, reflection-*on*-action, and reflection-*in*-action. Reflection-on-action relates to the time you take after completing an action (whether an interaction, lesson, or assignment). Reflection-in-action involves thinking about what you are doing *while* you are doing it. Killion and Todnem (1991) suggest that there is a third type of reflection known, as one may predict, as reflection-*for*-action which, naturally, addresses planning for future actions.

Examples of Reflection

The following are excerpts from reflections of students, two in their first pre-professional courses, and the other a student teacher. As you read these selections, refer back to the goals of reflection and the models of reflection noted in this chapter. In our first example from Katie, she shares both her excitement and her fears about her first clinical. Additionally, she includes some philosophical goals that she is developing.

SAMPLE ARTIFACT
PRE-PROFESSIONAL REFLECTION
Katie Levernier
Fall, 1999

MY CLINICAL EXPERIENCE

My clinical experience in West Aurora was a wonderful experience for me. I not only learned from my cooperating teacher and other staff members, but my students taught me most of all. I learned classroom management, positive reinforcements, motivations, levels that the children should be at, and about each child academically and socially. I didn't know exactly what to expect entering this clinical. Would the teacher consider me an inconvenience or would she appreciate my help and strive to help me learn all that she had to offer? Do I sit and wait to be asked to help, or do I dive right in without being asked? These and many other questions pondered my mind as I drove to West Aurora on my very first day as a teacher. I was excited and nervous, giddy and extremely tired. I was prepared for anything and by the end of my first day very satisfied and excited for more. From the moment I entered the classroom Miss Larson, my cooperating teacher, made me feel extremely welcome to ask questions, get involved with the students and their work, and even offer ideas and suggestions I may have. I walked around answering all kinds of questions, did math and reading tests individually with the children, and even walked them to gym class. I knew from this day forward that I was headed in the correct path for my life.

…My classroom is going to be a positive learning environment where my children grow not only academically, but socially as well. I want to have an open and loving rapport with my students. I want to know them academically, yet also on an individual status. I feel to be a great teacher you must understand where the child is coming from and the types of situations the child may be dealing with. For example, if John's parents are getting divorced this will definitely take a toll on his school work, his temper control, and even his motivation levels. As a teacher I want to be aware of any conditions in or out of school so that I can create the best learning environment for that student.

This next reflection from Stephanie includes important information on her clinical experience such as age, cultural and socio-economic backgrounds of the students, and some explanation of the history of the school's language arts curriculum. Stephanie goes on to describe what she believes she will and will not choose to do when she is a teacher.

SAMPLE ARTIFACT
Stephanie Brenner
Clinical Reflections
November, 1999

My first clinical experience was in a fifth grade class in West Aurora's Smith Elementary School. The class consists of 30 students. There are sixteen girls and fourteen boys, all ten to eleven years old. Most are from lower to lower-middle class SES. The breakdown of ethnicities is as follows: 11 Mexican American students, 12 African Americans, 6 Caucasians, and one Asian American. This was my first experience in a classroom where the white children are the minority.

Before I discuss my cooperating teacher's framework, I should give some information about the recent history of the reading philosophy for the whole school. This is the first year my teacher, Mrs. M., taught fifth grade. The previous eleven years she taught at Smith, she had third grade classes. Three years ago the school took away the teachers' basal, shifting to the whole language approach to reading. The teachers had to come up with their own resources, ordering books from Scholastic and making lots of Xeroxes for worksheets from extension activity books. After some time, the teachers realized the students were just not learning how to read. Test scores even proved it.

…I want to try to…
- Incorporate more language arts into social studies and science. More thematic units would allow for a smoother flow throughout the day.

- Have several reward systems that are meaningful to the students. I know this creates extrinsic motivation, but at least there would be some motivation. For example, I would have a chart for spelling. For every A, a child gets a star. But, I would stress that it is a team effort. If the entire class can earn 300 stars before Christmas then they can have a pizza party or something else they choose as a class.
- Encourage students to write well by writing for an audience (besides me.) I would have the class create a newspaper biweekly (or to accompany a thematic unit.) Each child would have some sort of writing contribution (maybe switch off who writes the front page story) and the newspapers would be copied for the class and their parents to read.

I do not like…
- Being disorganized. I am generally a very organized person, but Mrs. M. was extremely disorganized. It sort of drove me nuts, but I was flexible. It did reinforce how important it is to be organized as a teacher because of all the paperwork I will deal with. Trying to locate papers and books wasted a great deal of time, not to mention it appears very unprofessional. I am sure she also misplaced some of the students' homework as well. She figured they did not turn it in and so they would have to redo it. Many times the students became understandably frustrated with her.
- Cram too many activities into too short of a time period. I think it would be more beneficial to the students (as well as the whole feeling of the classroom) to spend more focused, meaningful time on each activity rather than try to do all activities everyday and rush through them.
- Stretch out writing essays. I think it would be better to do an entire essay in one or two days. In my clinical classroom they took an entire week to write an essay. The first day would be brainstorming. The second and third days were interchanged because Ms. X was experimenting. One day would be for the introduction and the other day would be for the body. The fourth day was dedicated to the conclusion and the fifth involved editing and writing the formal copy to hand in. I felt like this was too broken up. The second day the students would have to brainstorm again to remember what they were writing about and by the end of the week they were very confused about which paragraphs went where. They got to the point where they did not even know what they were writing about…

In this final reflection, student teacher Joe takes a risk by showing a deep exploration of both his actions-or lack of them- and the reasons behind those actions. Fearless, honest attempts such as this indicate that he is willing to examine his choices even when they may reflect a less desirable side of him.

SAMPLE ARTIFACT
Joe Pourroy
Student Teacher Reflection
Spring, 1998

Embracing adversity is not a natural trait for me. I am able to give people space to be different, or see things differently, but I don't generally relish the friction that causes.

I am seldom in a position where I fight for my point of view. For as long as I can remember I seem to be a "fence sitter." Seeing the pros and cons of both sides produces a catatonic response that stifles action and conflict.

Social justice is one area that I am willing to risk adversity as a result of my actions. I seek the truth about the world and am willing to risk rejection in speaking that truth.

Artifact Rationales

A prime time to reflect upon your actions is when you are choosing artifacts for your professional portfolio. As you select the artifacts that best represent you, consider the following reflective questions:

- Why does this particular artifact appeal to you?
- What do you want those evaluating you to learn from this artifact?
- What qualities does this artifact reflect about you?
- What category would this artifact fall into?
- Have you covered this type of artifact enough that you don't really need to include anymore?
- What will you state about this artifact when discussing it with whomever is evaluating you?

Implications

Reflection-on-action, reflection-in-action, and reflection-for-action are all important when conveying how your experiences have affected you. Reflection-on-action occurs after an experience, reflection-in-action occurs while you are participating in the new experience, and reflection-for-action occurs when you plan for how to improve next time.

References

Arends, R. I., Winitzky, N.E., & Tannenbaum, M.D. (1998). *Exploring Teaching*. Boston: McGraw-Hill.

Arends, R.I. (1998). *Learning to Teach*. Boston: McGraw-Hill.

Borko, H., et al (1997). Student teaching portfolios: A tool for promoting reflective practice. *Journal of Teacher Education* 48 (5), 345-357.

Costantino, P.M. & De Lorenzo, M.N. (1998). *Developing a Professional Teaching Portfolio, A Guide for Educators.* College Park: University of Maryland.

Farris, P.J. (1999). *Teaching: Bearing the Torch, Second Edition.* Boston: McGraw-Hill.

Killion, J.P. & Todnem, G.R. (1991). A process for personal theory building. *Educational Leadership* 48 (6), 14-16.

Lyons, N. (1998). Reflection in teaching: Can it be developmental? A portfolio perspective. *Teacher Education Quarterly.* 25 (1), 115-127.

Sadker, M., and Sadker, D. (2000). *Teachers, Schools, & Society, Fifth Edition.* Boston: McGraw-Hill.

Schon, D.A. (1983). *The Reflective Practitioner*. New York: Basic Books.

Website Suggestions

This website from Mary Ellen Nevins of Kean College of New Jersey offers professional portfolio design advice specifically for preservice students majoring in education of students with hearing impairments.

http://www.educ.kent.edu/deafed/970108o.htm

NOTES

_____

_____

_____

_____

_____

_____

_____

_____

_____

_____

_____

_____

_____

_____

_____

_____

_____

My Philosophy of Education

Having been in the classroom for my first professional semester, I have learned thus far what education means to me. In the classroom I feel students need to learn socially, emotionally, physically, and intellectually. The most important aspect to be aware of is that no two children learn in the same way. Teachers have to be flexible and diverse in their methods. Using one method for the entire class will most often not be appropriate for every child. By varying teaching methods, the teacher will also help the students become aware of several methods of problem solving. These methods can in turn be used throughout their lives.

I feel what we teach children needs to be relevant to real life experiences. I have observed that when students know they will be using what they learn and they can relate it to something in their lives they will be more interested and more likely to remember what they have been taught. Socialization helps children become ready to be active citizens and workers in life. It is important to be able to work with others and by teaching this early in life, it will be much easier to continue throughout life, even when not in school.

I hope to be a teacher who is flexible in every aspect of my teaching methods. I want to expand my skills to meet the needs of every student. My goal is that my students will leave my classroom feeling they have learned lessons they can use throughout their lives. As a life long learner myself, I want to instill the same values in my students.

Chapter 6
Recognizing and Expressing Your Philosophy

"Teachers represent the collective wisdom of our culture and insist on maintaining the integrity of the methods, substance and structures of disciplinary knowledge. In the face of pressures to portray knowledge in weak and diluted forms, they remain firm. Their role, however, is not just to reinforce the status quo. Rather, appreciative of the fact that there are multiple perspectives and interpretations in each discipline, accomplished teachers encourage students to question prevailing canons and assumptions to help them think for themselves."
(National Board for Professional Teaching Standards, 1999)

This quote from the National Board for Professional Teaching Standards eloquently defines their definition of the role of teachers. Their definition is comprehensive and thus difficult to argue. Your philosophy of teaching will be one of the multiple perspectives to which they refer. When considering the subject(s) you will teach, your philosophy will be reflected in your actions which, in turn, are driven by your beliefs in the following areas:

- Why should your subject be taught?
- What are the desired outcomes for your students following your lesson?
- What impacts will the knowledge that students gain have on society?
- How will you present the lesson?
- What is the best way for your students to learn?
- When are students developmentally ready to learn your subject?
- How will you assess students' mastery of the subject?
- What is your style of classroom management?
- To what extent will parents be involved in your lessons?
- Will you assign homework? If so, for what purpose?

As you can imagine, the possible philosophical questions are innumerable. These ten questions are but the tip of the iceberg of educational philosophies. In this chapter we'll explore some of the better-known philosophies of teaching with the goal of guiding you to recognize the descriptions of some of your own philosophies.

Basic Educational Philosophies
In your foundation of education courses, you will receive more extensive instruction on the intricacies and history of various educational philosophies. For the purpose of this text, we will only need a brief overview of the most well-known educational philosophies. The first of these is Idealism.

Idealism

Idealism, the oldest known philosophy, is associated with Plato, Descartes, Kant, and Spinoza, among others. Although idealists are often conservative, Friedrich Froebel, the founder of the kindergarten, was a liberal. Idealists tend to believe that students are all capable of being positive, contributing members of society, and that discipline matters can be handled "in-house" by simply talking rationally with the disruptive student. Idealistic teachers believe that students should find joy in education because they seek the truth, and that the curriculum should be based on cultural heritage (Farris, 1999).

Realism

Realists, like their predecessors Aristotle, Comenius, Pestalozzi, Herbart, and Montessori, believe that lessons must be structured, realistic, and focus on accuracy and accountability (Farris, 1999). Instructors whose roots are in Realism tend to be strong, consistent disciplinarians whose rules and consequences are posted and discussed on the first day of class, then enforced fairly and firmly throughout the school year.

Perennialism

If you see your role in education as that of a moral, intellectual authority figure, you may find your beliefs lie within the philosophy of Perennialism. Most of the schools in western society are based on Perennialism (Arends, 1998), which means that the students and teachers have pre-determined, respectful roles they must play in order to prepare students to fulfill their duties in society. Perennialist programs often use classical literature, and their curricula require students to undergo challenging, rigorous courses. Like Robert Hutchins and Mortimer Adler, professors in the college of education who are perennialists will focus more on academic subjects than on individual needs or aesthetics.

Progressivism

Perhaps the most well known proponent of Progressivism is John Dewey. Progressivists believe that students must be prepared to live in an ever-changing society. One strong proponent of Dewey's theories was Francis Parker who, rather than dictating the belief system to be emulated, encouraged his teachers to think critically and creatively. Cooperative learning, hands-on activities, intrinsic rewards, and the role of teacher as facilitator rather than expert are all basic tenets of Progressivism.

Pragmatism

Much of what you learned in your own kindergarten through 12th grade experience probably reflected the values of pragmatism. Charles Peirce, a 19th and 20th century mathematician and scientist, was a pragmatist, as was John Dewey before he began the experimentalism and progressivism movements. Pragmatists tend to be problem solvers who value use of the scientific method. They may use quality literature to teach both language arts and social studies in integrated units. Students of pragmatists will be encouraged to apply their knowledge in authentic, hands-on experiences.

Existentialism

Do you find yourself considering all angles of a problem, with the realization that the implications of your decision will be far-reaching? Do you often rebel against traditional approaches to teaching? If you, like your predecessors Jean-Paul Sartre and Friedrich Nietzsche, feel that you must always be free to choose and be responsible for your choices, you are affiliated with the existentialist philosophy. Existentialism is difficult to define because to define it would be to confine it—which would make it no longer existentialism. Existentialist educators focus on empowering their students with individual freedom, and will stress arts and literature over math and science. (Farris, 1999).

Essentialism

Teachers who believe that the primary purpose of their curriculum is to transmit useful skills are considered to be followers of Essentialism. A good example of Essentialism is the publication *A Nation at Risk*, published by the National Commission on Excellence in Education in 1983 to promote the implementation of tougher academic standards. Essentialism is also reflected in the current trend toward discussion of adopting national teaching standards. Essentialists believe that the emphasis in public schools should be on academics, with each subject taught separately, and with high levels of time on task. The role of schools is to create successful citizens (Arends, 1998). Students taught by essentialists can expect to be tested often for mastery, and to experience "skill and drill" lessons. (Farris, 1999.)

Experimentalism

Along with progressivism, John Dewey also founded the idea of Experimentalism. Experimentalists stress the use of science in schools, see the teacher as the most important component in the classroom, and believe that all subject matter should be connected both to other subjects and to the students' home lives. Experimentalist educators will focus on child-centered activities, and will allow much time for play because children need to play in order to learn to compete and to cooperate. (Farris, 1999.)

Social Reconstructionism

Finally, there is Social Reconstructionism, sometimes referred to simply as Reconstructionism. Reconstructionists believe that the function of schools is to teach students to examine social problems and, ultimately, to change society for the better. The theory that schools should be a model of the way we believe the world should be is a good example of Reconstructionism. (Arends, 1998).

Expressing Your Philosophy: an Example

In the following essay, Deanna describes how she came to the conclusion that she holds an essentialist philosophy of education.

SAMPLE ARTIFACT
Deanna Biscan
Spring, 1997

Philosophy of Education

After completing the philosophy questionnaire on page 404, I scored highest as an Essentialist. But after reading the chapter and becoming familiar with what I believe is correct, I strongly agree with Progressivism and Behaviorism. Although, an eclectic approach to teaching is what I hope to accomplish.

Progressivism, which is similar to Existentialism, involves the freedom of experiencing different views and outlooks on life and the learning process. Extracurricular activities and classes help the students get a look at and experience different fields. This is an advantage for deciding possible career choices. Progressivism is based on the belief that lessons must seem relevant to the students in order for them to learn. The curriculum of a progressivist school is built around the personal experiences, interests and needs of the students. The teacher must do whatever it takes to make the students learn the material in an understanding way to them.

Existentialism goes a little further and believes in human free will. This philosophy is not American-like. Students in existentialist schools are allowed to control their own education. They are encouraged to understand and appreciate their uniqueness and to assume responsibility for their actions. This is an effective philosophy if the student is trustworthy and uses it in a positive way. Too much freedom and no real discipline could be useless in educating the students. It depends upon each particular student and his/her effort.

Behaviorism is based on the views that human beings are primarily the product of their environment and that children can become moral, intelligent people if they are rewarded for proper behavior. Behaviorists break down material into small lessons, test the students after each lesson, and reward the students for proper responses on the tests. Effective Behaviorism motivates the students to learn, not to train or control them. At K.I.D.'s CLUB, the day care center I work at, we have a jar that marbles are placed into for good behavior. When the jar is full, the kids will receive a free pizza party. This is an example of a Behaviorist approach for the students to behave well.

As the role of a teacher, I would choose an eclectic approach favoring Progressivism, Existentialism, and Behaviorism. All philosophies are important in one way or another, yet these three are definitely of my preference. On pages 429 and 432, two teachers caught my attention and I agreed with their statements. Marcus Washington said that we need to offer students an alternative to teaching. They need to learn how to think and solve problems using real life situations. We learn by living. Margaret Nava stated that who we are is determined by our environment and students learning should be monitored. This would help the teacher see what the students have mastered and what they need to relearn. Moving on to the next material should only be done if all students are familiar with the present subject.

In my store evaluation report I described the types of materials and supplies that I would use for my classroom. I will try my hardest to make the students learn in an easy and interesting way to them. The type of teacher depends upon the amount of information learned. I do not want to be boring or monotonous, but creative and interesting to listen and learn from. On page 61 in the textbook, there is a list of ideas for teaching. I would consider all of these and hope that they will be successful when teaching the students. These activities and skills for teaching will most likely excite and motivate the children to learn.

Recall and recognition are both very important testing procedures. Although recognition is highly preferred by most students, recall seems to determine exactly what the student knows on their own. Students shouldn't have to memorize material for tests, they should understand it. This way the test or exam will be much easier for them to complete with confidence. All tests and questions should be valid. Competence and performance should be considered when making the next test. You want the students to be challenged, but not tricked when taking tests. All students learn in different ways, which needs to be considered when reviewing and issuing tests. For each subject, I would include a pop quiz, an expected quiz, a review session and the final test with extra credit available. This way the students are always having to study and keep on task with their work. The results on the final test will count the most and will hopefully lead to high scores.

When transferring to another school, I will research the background and philosophy of teaching there. After making sure that all my credits transfer over and the classes I'm interested in are available to me, then I will definitely consider the school. I don't want to be taught or trained in a different belief or philosophy that I don't agree with. I hope to expand my knowledge and teaching skills at the transfer school I attend. Hopefully I will be lucky enough to become an elementary teacher and teach in a school with a well-organized curriculum that I will be glad to follow.

A Modern View of Educational Philosophies

Stamm and Wactler (1997) have come up with a more simple method of defining professional philosophies. In their text, *Philosophy of Education Workbook*, Stamm and Wactler outline four main teaching philosophical orientations or approaches:

- Executive Approach
- Humanist Approach
- Classicist Approach
- Informationist Approach

Each approach describes five identifying qualities. These qualities are described as roles played by the teacher, by the student, by the environment, by the focus of the class, and by the emphasis of the class. For example, an Informationist Approach would see the teacher as interpreter, the student as participant, the environment as technologically centered, the focus on communications and community, and the emphasis on the meaning of information (Stamm & Wactler, p.13.) Because these four approaches are relatively new, be sure to explain them if you refer to them in your portfolio.

Examples of Statements of Philosophy

As you read the following excerpts of students' philosophies, take notes on the key words that guide you in determining which philosophies these students express. Afterwards, compare your interpretations with ours. Look for our interpretations following the references at the end of the chapter.

"...My classroom is going to be a positive learning environment where my children grow not only academically, but socially as well. I want to have an open and loving rapport with my students. I want to know them academically, yet also on an individual status. I feel to be a great teacher you must understand where the child is coming from and the types of situations the child may be dealing with." —Katie

"I also will always remember how well Mrs. C. was organized. That is something that is important to me. She was also very good at explaining the day's activities to the children so that they knew what was going to happen during the day. She always tried to involve them in the decision-making process. She definitely used a literacy framework. She was always finding what worked best with her students." —Liz

"(I feel my best achievements in this experience were...)Noticing that students have improved and really try harder after I've worked individually with them. When I see understanding in them." —Deanna

How Do These Philosophies Apply to You?

Imagine that you are principal of a brand-new school. You want to hire educators whose philosophies either reflect your own, or are compatible with yours. What characteristics will those teachers have? Take a moment to write in your notes the questions you, as principal, would ask, and also recognize the answers you would most like to hear. This reflection will help you to identify your own teaching philosophy.

Next, review your instinctual answers to the ten questions listed at the beginning of this chapter. After you've reviewed your answers, read again through the philosophy descriptions and determine which philosophies your answers reflect. It is entirely possible to hold a combination of philosophies; and you should also bear in mind that as you gain new experiences and frames of reference, your philosophies might very well change.

Implications

New teachers may not realize that they hold definable philosophies of education. With focused reflection, it is possible to identify some of the basic tenets of your own philosophy. The main philosophies covered in this chapter were Idealism, Realism, Perennialism, Progressivism, Essentialism, Existentialism, Pragmatism, Experimentalism, and Social Reconstructionism. Most public schools reflect the philosophies of Pragmatism and Perennialism; however, the strive toward national teaching standards and accountability is an example of Essentialism.

Jill Stamm and Caroline Wactler (1997) have developed a more simple, "user-friendly" system to determine teaching philosophies. Their four teaching philosophies are executive, classicist, humanist, and informationist. Each philosophy has five main components: roles played by the teacher, the students, the environment, the focus, and the emphasis. It is important to realize that whatever philosophical tendencies you recognize in yourself today are not necessarily permanent—experience and students' needs will both impact your beliefs.

References

Arends, R.I., et al (1998). *Exploring Teaching*. Boston: McGraw-Hill.

Farris, P.J. (1999). *Teaching, Bearing the Torch, 2nd Edition*. Boston: McGraw-Hill.

National Board for Professional Teaching Standards (1999). *What Teachers Should Know and Be Able To Do*. Southfield, MI: NBPTS.

Stamm, J. & Wactler, C. (1997). *Philosophy of Education Workbook, Writing a Statement of Beliefs and Practices*. Boston: McGraw-Hill.

Interpreting Katie, Liz, and Deanna

Katie's themes of a child-centered approach in which she strives to meet individual needs indicates that she is expressing philosophies of idealism and experimentalism.

Liz's admiration of her cooperating teacher's ability to provide routine and structure and still involve her students in decision-making shows an interesting blend of the ideas of realism and existentialism.

Finally, Deanna's comment on how her students' effort improved suggests that her philosophy is centered in progressivism.

Website Suggestions

For more information on the NBPTS, go to

www.nbpts.org

For information on a book showing that John Dewey's progressive education philosophy demands a pragmatic home school pedagogy, go to

http://www.publicfamily.com/

For more information on educational philosophies, go to

http://www.wcl.american.edu/PUB/handbook/philosophies.html

NOTES

_____

_____

_____

_____

_____

_____

_____

_____

_____

_____

_____

_____

_____

_____

_____

_____

_____

Dear Parents,

Welcome to the 2000-2001 school year at Jones Middle School! We on the seventh grade team are looking forward to a year full of adventure, fun, and, of course, learning. Just a few reminders to start us all off on the right track...

1)   We believe that our role as educators is to guide our students on a journey. By presenting them with current, relevant information through a variety of presentation modes in a cooperative, supportive learning environment, we hope to engage all of our students in the learning process and encourage them all to develop study habits that foster life-long learning.

2)   Be sure to read over the school mission and the expectations and consequences on p. 2 and p. 5 in the student handbook. You'll need to tear out, sign, and return the form on page 6 stating that you have read them and agree to them.

3)   Remember that we all—staff, parents, and students—are working together to provide the best possible education for your children.

4)   If you have any questions or concerns, please contact us at 555-1234 between the hours of 8 a.m. and 3 p.m. Be sure to leave a message explaining when we can reach you with the best phone numbers.

Thank you in advance for an excellent year!

Sincerely,
Ms. Lacalla, Mr. Ivory, Mrs. Ruiz, Mr. Janssen, and Miss Smith

Chapter 7
Proactive Classroom Management

Whether you are a first-year educator about to embark on the marvelous journey of teaching second graders or a veteran educator beginning your twentieth year of enlightening high schoolers, you will need to have a classroom management plan. Your plan will include your expectations of behavior, rules, planned consequences for following (or not following) the rules, and a record-keeping method of monitoring such compliance or lack of compliance.

The best use of classroom management is as a proactive, preventative tool. Anticipate problems, be sensitive to students' needs[1], and keep parents, administrators, and colleagues well-informed.

Parents

Parent are an incredible wealth of information and should be regarded and treated as valuable team members. They are well-versed in their children's moods, preferences, nutrition, concerns, and interests. Unfortunately, parents are often the last to know when their child is failing; and, even more unfortunately, may also be the last to know when their child has done something commendable. It is vital to include parents in the team of experts working together for the sake of the student. There are many ways to document parent contact, and just as many reasons to do so. By staying in contact with parents you are demonstrating your desire to provide your students with the best possible educational support system. You also show your ability to establish rapport and to work cooperatively to solve problems. Additionally, documenting parent contacts protects you in disputes, communicates to your administrators that you value your rapport with the parents, and reminds you when and why you have contacted parents.

One way to document parent contact is with a contact log. Even when student teaching, you will benefit from contacts with parents. Keep records of your contacts with a log such as the following; however, if you include the log in your portfolio, be careful to change names, dates, and locations to protect confidentiality.

---

[1] For more information on meeting students' needs, see Chapter 8, Lesson Plans and Curricular Modifications.

```
┌─────────────────────────────────────────────────────────────────────┐
│ Parent Contact Sheet                                                  │
│ Date    Parent's Name  Child's Name  Method of Contact   Reason for Contact   Outcome │
│                                                                       │
│ _____   │
│                                                                       │
│ _____   │
│                                                                       │
│ _____   │
│                                                                       │
│ _____   │
│                                                                       │
│ _____   │
│                                                                       │
└─────────────────────────────────────────────────────────────────────┘
```

Another tried and true method to document contacts is to keep each of your students' names, addresses, and phone numbers on separate index cards. This way you can simply pull out the student's card, have the parent's name, address, and number readily available, and document the contact. With the advances in computer technology, there are also numerous ways to keep records in your computer. Regardless the method, it is vital to document the "good" reasons for contact as well as the "bad" ones. Principals and other disciplinarians will appreciate your willingness to work with parents as well as your ability to keep records of important parental contacts. Include in your portfolio the documentation record sheets you've created.

Colleagues and Administrators

Your colleagues and administrators, too, are impacted daily by your classroom management style. In elementary school, or in fact, in any level of school, how you discipline your students will be compared by the students and their parents to how other teachers manage discipline. It is important to combine your individual style with a consistent message conveyed by the staff as a whole. In middle school or high school, your team or department may have a policy regarding discipline. When you apply for a teaching position, ask for a copy of their student handbook. Consider placing in your portfolio a copy of the school's mission statement and/or your team or departmental policy. Comment on this artifact and state how you plan to enforce these beliefs.

The following mission statement and behavior management model are from a middle school student handbook. In your notes, write some ideas on how you would express your plan to uphold and enforce these ideals.

Mission Statement
The staff at Jones Middle School is committed to establishing and maintaining an equitable and dynamic educational experience designed to meet the unique physical, emotional, and social needs of the adolescent learner. We realize that a strong home-school-community relationship, emphasizing good communication is crucial to the successful completion of our mission.

Behavior Management
After an introductory paragraph, the following expectations and consequences are delineated:

Expectations for behavior include:
1) Follow directions the first time given.
2) Listen respectfully when others are speaking.
3) Work in class without disturbing others.
4) Respect others' rights, feelings, and property.
5) Conduct yourself in a manner that promotes safety for all.

Consequences for misbehavior include:
1) Warning
2) Teacher detention with parent or guardian contact (written/phone)
3) School detention with parent or guardian contact (written/phone)
4) Team meeting with the student
5) Team meeting with the student and parent/guardian
6) Referral to the principal for further disciplinary action, including suspension
Severe Clause: Students may be referred to the office at any time for severe disruptions.

Communication and Management Styles

Just as there are many variations of educational philosophies[2], so too are there many variations of classroom management styles. Even in your earliest clinical experiences, you will be experimenting to find your own style of communicating and enforcing your expectations. Some aspects of classroom management may also be considered to be modifications for students with special needs; for example, if Donita learns better by working in a quiet place, she will benefit from your allowing her to move to a corner to work. By allowing Donita to move, you are also practicing preventive classroom management.

Talk to your cooperating teachers and your instructors to find out the ways that they use preventive classroom management. In your portfolio, include your written observations of these professionals' methods and your ideas of what you would like to try.

---

[2] See Chapter 6, Recognizing and Expressing Your Philosophy.

Sometimes utilizing proactive communication is just plain fun. There are myriad reproducible resources available in teacher stores, catalogs, and online. One excellent resource is the *Classroom Teacher's Survival Guide: Practical strategies, management techniques, and reproducibles for new and experienced teachers* (Partin, 1995.)

Displaying Your Skills

Parents often cite school discipline as one of their greatest concerns, and principals have unfortunate task of dismissing otherwise bright and talented educators because of their inability to effectively create a positive learning environment. You have already seen sample letters, contact forms, and school discipline plans. What other items would be creative ways to display your knowledge of classroom management? Write in your notes some ideas, then read on.

Letters of Thanks

Parents and students are both likely to write you letters of thanks when you are able to help a student with a problem. Students appreciate having someone objective and caring to tell their troubles to, and parents often will feel that all their child really needed was a fresh start with a new face. Regardless the circumstance, letters thanking you for the difference you've made are excellent artifacts to include.

Another idea is to include letters of thanks that you've written to students. Such artifacts demonstrate that you value your students as equal partners in the classroom. Consider keeping a supply of fun stationery and post-it notes for occasions such as this. Like any documents that include students' names, obtain written parent permission before including them in your portfolio. Note this sample from a student teacher of students with behavior disorders:

January 28, 2000

Dear Tsui Lin:

I want to thank you for how hard you worked today to keep your temper. I know that sometimes LaJuana works really hard to try to "get your goat," and you did a marvelous job today of choosing not to engage with her. I saw you use your skills of moving away from the problem and of asking for help when you needed it. You've come a long way, and I hope you're as proud of yourself as I am of you!
Have a great weekend, you deserve it!

Sincerely,
Ms. Vasquez

In Ms. Vasquez's note, her praise is specific. Tsui-Lin avoided making a tough situation worse and in so doing, demonstrated her mastery of one of her behavioral goals. If you include artifacts such as this, be sure that they demonstrate both your communication skills and your knowledge of students' needs.

Certificates

You may attend professional conferences while you're in school, take one-day seminars at your college, or complete courses in classroom management. If there are not certificates available, ask for letters of recommendation from the facilitators or instructors.

Classroom Rules

You may be asked to create a discipline plan for your student teaching experience. Word it in a positive, proactive way, make it attractive and simple to read, and copy it for your portfolio. See the following classroom rules the author implemented in her class for students with behavior disorders. Note that the word "not" is <u>not</u> used; it is much more effective to state your expectations positively. Most experts suggest that classroom rules be simply stated and number only a few. It is best practice to have the rules in mind when you start the school year, but still discuss with and receive input from your students about the rules. Students often have good ideas and enjoy sharing in decision-making. When they feel ownership in the rules, students are more likely to help enforce them.

CLASSROOM RULES

1) Do no harm.

2) Respect others' property, space, and feelings.

3) Come on time and prepared to work.

4) Ask for help appropriately and when needed.

5) Instead of "I can't," say, "I will try, but I need help."

6) Follow all school rules.

In addition to the set of rules, include a rationale for them, such as:

These rules were sent home with the "welcome to the school year" letters the parents received in the first week. I felt it was important to make "do no harm" and "respect others…" the first two rules because they are all encompassing—do nothing to harm others or yourself either physically or emotionally. Rules 3, 4, and 5 address students' academic behaviors—we are all here to give our best effort. Finally, "follow all school rules" covers any rules that the student handbook may include.

Seating Charts and Floor Plans

As you become familiar with both your learning and teaching style and the needs and preferences of your students, you'll find that you will often be looking critically at the layout of your classroom. Considerations such as whether to use rows of desks, pods or clusters of desks, or tables and chairs will take into account which students will benefit from being together and which will be more comfortable and able to attend by sitting alone. Additionally, components out of your control such as electrical outlets, climate control, doors, windows, lights, and bulletin boards all must be taken into account when you are designing the layout of your room.

In your portfolio, include a floor plan of your classroom and write a rationale for the organization. If you have not yet had the opportunity to rearrange a classroom, observe several styles of classrooms and take notes on what you think are the best ideas. Draw diagrams to help you remember these ideas.

Case Studies

Every teacher has at least one student that he/she wishes for a magic wand to "cure." The student may be brilliant but lacking in motivation, be reluctant to speak but a gifted writer, be better one-on-one than in groups, or be an incredible distraction to others whenever present. There is a key to success for every student, and sometimes regular classroom teachers are capable of finding and using the key in time to make a difference. One valuable artifact is a narrative case study of a particular student. The first step is to either obtain parental permission to use the student's name and experiences, or take precautions to protect the confidentiality rights of that student. Next, observe and document several sessions with the student. Note times of day, subjects, types of behavior, and what appears to trigger the behavior. After identifying the behavior, setting, and possible reasons, describe what you plan to try to help the student and your rationale. The subsequent step will be describing the outcome of your intervention and your beliefs concerning the reasons for the outcome. Finally, follow-up with more observations after the intervention and new behaviors have become routine.

Positive Experiences with Students

Just as there is always at least one student to worry you, there will be countless students who delight you. It is important to focus--both in your experiences and in your portfolio--on the positive aspects of your classroom. Ask yourself: what are you doing right that is bringing out the best in these students? How can you maintain the positive attitudes of the appropriately-behaving students when you must take time to deal with those who are struggling?

One enjoyable, even therapeutic method of keeping track of successes is to maintain a good news journal. Every day, even after the roughest of days, take time to write down all the good things you can think of that happened in class that day. They may be truly unique experiences such as a student's first A on a test, or they may be less obvious, such as a student's choosing to opt out of engaging in a bad situation and ask for your help instead. Model the understanding that everyone's choices matter by including reflections on your own actions; for example, note that you chose to eat a healthy lunch, that you got your papers all graded before you watched a video, or that you chose to speak politely and assertively when you felt angry. Once a week, or whatever schedule your class feels comfortable with, read aloud the recent entries. You'll find that students listen eagerly to hear themselves mentioned, and you may also receive suggestions from students about what to include in the journal.

If you choose to include in your portfolio excerpts from your good news journal, remember that even good news must be treated as confidential information--students may only be identified with parental permission.

Implications
This chapter has suggested the following artifacts for your portfolio:
- Parent contact sheets
- School mission statements and excerpts from student handbook
- Certificates of workshops and seminars attended
- Classroom rules
- Rationale for rules
- Letters to and from parents (with confidentiality addressed)
- Excerpts from a good news journal
- Seating charts and classroom floor plans
- Case Studies

Classroom management is a necessary, vital component of any good teacher's best practices. Principals and other head disciplinarians will need to be fully informed whenever you expect them to enforce consequences. Parents need-and have the right-to be kept abreast of their child's appropriate or inappropriate behavioral tendencies. Colleagues will need you to help support and convey a unity of values in classroom management decisions.

References
Partin, Ronald (1995). *Classroom Teacher's Survival Guide: Practical Strategies, Management Techniques, and Reproducibles for New and Experienced Teachers.* West Nyack, NY: The Center for Applied Research in Education.

Recommended Reading
Kidder, T. (1998). Among Schoolchildren. Houghton Mifflin Co.

Paley, V.P. (1992). You Can't Say, You Can't Play. Harvard University Press.

Website Suggestions:

For information and strategies for dealing with students who have attention disorders in the classroom, go to

http://www.oise.utoronto.ca/~stuserv/teaching/cmanage.htm

For *Free Gradebook Software* -or- a *Complete Classroom Organizer* to help teachers communicate with students and parents, go to

http://www.thinkwave.com/

To see a classroom management menu, go to

http://ss.uno.edu/ss/teachdevel/ClassMan/ClassManagMenu.html

NOTES

_____

_____

_____

_____

_____

_____

_____

_____

_____

_____

_____

_____

_____

_____

_____

_____

_____

_____

From the Real World

In Chapter 3, Michael Devereaux shared D his advice on best practices when creating a portfolio. He continues...

I feel our district uses an excellent interview practice. We do not interview in isolation. We will compose a team for interviewing. The team will consist of the building principal, another teacher at the same grade level, perhaps a teaching assistant who may work with the person, other principal(s). During the interview the candidate(s) will present a 10-minute lesson of their choice on a given topic, e.g.: *"You are a 3rd grade teacher. Present a 10-minute language arts lesson."* This is really where an excellent candidate will shine. However, a candidate is not hired on presenting a lesson only. Another important part of the interview is the written part. Interviewers are asked to focus on spelling, grammar, and content—in that order. (NOTE: ALL interviewers are given an orientation prior to the actual interviews.)

What to never/ever do during an interview: DO NOT display extremes. DO be humorous, but not obnoxious. DO explain yourself, but not too lengthily. DO be calm, but not sloppy. DO be professional, but not aloof. Again, DO NOT DISPLAY EXTREMES.

Things I look for in a beginning teacher are those qualities listed above. I also focus and ask about being a team player, a collaborative teacher, and above all someone who is kind and caring to children. It is called the "art" of teaching.

There are three types of questions that I ask during an interview: informational; situational; and philosophical. The situational questions can be very interesting and revealing about a candidate.

The main advice I give to those who ask me is to be yourself. Get hired because of what and who you are. If you are a kind, caring person, then display that. If you are a grumpy, short-tempered individual, then become something other than a teacher.

Chapter 8
Lesson Plans and Curricular Modifications

The longer you teach, the better you will be able to judge the prior knowledge of your students, the appropriateness of curriculum, and the amount of time to allow for lessons and activities. As a pre-service teacher, it is important to work at honing these skills. Whenever you are given the opportunity to develop and present a lesson, be sure to write out a detailed outline of the lesson. Save photos, worksheets you've created, and get permission from students' parents to keep copies of their work in your portfolio.

Artifacts to Include

When choosing items for the lesson plan components of your portfolio, choose plans that you have had an opportunity to try out on students. Include the specific plan written-out step by step, and follow the plan with a reflection on how it went when you presented it. Some ideas for artifacts to include in this section are[1]:

- Bibliography of trade books you will use
- Lists of established basal series you've experienced
- Bibliography and abstract of articles you've read
- Lesson plan you've seen someone else implement with a reference to that person and an explanation of what you like about it
- Your own lesson plan followed by a reflection of how the lesson went
- Copies of worksheets, study guides, and assessment tools you've created

Sample Lesson Plan Artifacts

The following artifacts were created by students for their sophomore and junior clinical experiences. As you read through each plan and its following reflection, be thinking about how you would change the lesson. Also consider what issues this text has addressed concerning reflection, and determine what you would do to make the reflection more in-depth (reflection-on-action and –for-action.)

---

[1] For other ideas of artifacts to include in this section, see Chapter 4 on how to arrange your portfolio according to a set of standards.

Honors Program Lesson Plan

Book: The Dark at the Top of the Stairs

BACKGROUND:
This is review/practice. The students have already done similar activities in the past.

STUDENTS:
There is a wide range of abilities in the classroom. There are very advanced students in the class, compared to others, so this should be a good activity for all of the students. The class consists of 25 students.

OBJECTIVES:
- The students will identify the characters in the book.
- The students will identify the setting of the book.
- The students will display understanding of the story by writing predictions for the ending of the story.
- The students will demonstrate understanding of the main characters by writing a simulated journal of the ending of the story.

ANTICIPATORY SET:
After showing the cover and the title, ask the students what they think the book will be about:
"What does the title make you think of?"
"What do you think the main characters are?"
"Today you will be writing the ending of the story. While I am reading the story, I want you to think of some predictions for the ending in your heads. You will be writing these predictions when I am finished."

METHODS, PROCEDURES, ACTIVITIES:
1)   Ask the anticipatory set before reading.
2)   Read the book, stopping to ask the key questions below at the correct spots in the book, either discussing as a whole class or in "pair and share":
- Who are the main characters so far?
- What are their names?
- Where do the mice live?
- What are the mice going to do tomorrow in the morning?
- What do the mice think lives at the top of the stairs?
- What do you think is at the top of the stairs?
- What is your prediction for the ending of the story?

MODELING:
To model the predictions, I will make my own on the overhead. I will share my ending with the class, in both written and verbal manners.

CHECKS FOR UNDERSTANDING:
1) The students will verbally answer key questions throughout the reading by sharing with the whole class or in "pair and share."
2) The students will make accurate predictions while writing in their journals by recording the prediction and a proof of their reasoning.

MATERIALS:
Book: The Dark at the Top of the Stairs
Journals (each student will have one)
Writing utensils
Overhead projector and pens

GUIDED PRACTICE:
I will go over some of the students' predictions with them.
I will write a prediction for the ending on the overhead.

INDEPENDENT PRACTICE:
The students will write their own predictions for the ending of the story in their journals. They will be written as simulated journals.

ASSESSMENT:
The students' journals will be collected and read. Comments will be written as a response to each child's prediction.
There will also be an informal assessment by asking the key questions during reading of the story.

CLOSURE:
For closure, I will have some students read their endings to the class. I will read the ending of the book and ask whose predictions were right. Students will turn in their journals.

Heather has designed an outstanding lesson plan for her language arts clinical experience. However, like any lesson plan, this needs some fine-tuning. Take a moment to jot down in your notes your ideas on how you would improve this plan, then read on to see some suggestions.

Suggestions (in order of appearance):

1) Heather failed to correctly cite the children's book. Every university bookstore sells guides on how to correctly cite references. Find out what style your college prefers, and use it well. The most often used styles of citation are APA and MLA.

2) In describing the students, Heather fails to specify the grade and age of the students. We also do not know the socio-economic, gender, or cultural characteristics of the students.

3) Although we can gather from further information in the plan that Heather will stop reading aloud before the end of the story, she does not explicitly say so; neither does she explain just where she will stop and why.

4) In these days of embracing diversity, it is important to include some ideas on modifications for students with diverse learning needs and abilities. Three examples with respect to this lesson are:

- Students who have difficulty with written expression may be allowed to dictate their responses to a teacher, a study buddy, or an aide.
- Students may wish to draw a picture of the ending instead of writing it out.
- Students may wish to act out their predicted endings in a mini-Readers' Theater activity.

An important aspect of designing lessons is your reflections on how the lessons went. As we've already discussed, administrators look for teachers who examine their successes and/or failures with lessons, then plan for the future. Here is Heather's reflection:

SAMPLE ARTIFACT
Heather Taylor

Honors Program Read-Aloud Journal Lesson

The lesson for the read-aloud that I did went great. The students absolutely loved it. I began by asking the anticipatory set, and the students responded with so many different answers. While I read, the entire class was silent, which is a very rare occasion, and all of the students listened eagerly. I asked the key questions as I read, and the students were also able to answer those correctly. I wrote some information about the book, such as the characters' names, the setting, etc., to help the students follow along easier. I also made sure to spend a little extra time to show the pictures that went along with each page.

After I stopped at the point in the book where planned, the students gave me some of their predictions for the ending of the story. They spent about 15 minutes writing their predictions as if they were the characters in the book. Then, I collected the journals, and asked some students to share their predictions with the class.

To close the lesson, I read the rest of the book to the class, and we discussed it together. I also wrote short comments in each of the journals. It appeared that the majority of the students were able to come up with accurate predictions that were justified by their proof, while a couple students had nothing but the title written in their journals.

Overall, I think this lesson went really well, and I think that the students really enjoyed it.

Heather's excitement over the success of her lesson is contagious: any administrator would be pleased for her and would want to see more of her ideas in action. However, there is an omission in this reflection. What's missing? Write in your notes, then read on.

What's Missing?

Heather forgot to include her ideas on how to improve the lesson next time. One opportunity for such a reflection is her mention of the students who had nothing but the title written in their journals. Bringing up these students is a wonderful lead-in to how to make the lesson more accessible to all her students. She could suggest modifications to support students with learning needs or students who are not motivated to participate in the activity. The failure of these students to complete the assignment prompts Heather to ask questions such as:

- What could I have done differently to reach them all?
- Should I have circulated the room to monitor comprehension while students were responding in their journals?
- Why didn't the students ask me for help?
- Is this an unusual behavior for these students? I should ask their teacher.
- How can I approach the students in a non-threatening, concerned manner?

Aside from the concern for the students who did not finish, Heather could give some specific examples of student responses. She could also include some criticism of her delivery of the lesson—did it flow smoothly? Did she fumble with the pages? Could all students see the pictures? No one is perfect, and it is important to note in your reflections ways to improve.

Ryan, another junior education major, has an engaging account of the presentation of his lesson. Read Ryan's lesson plan and reflection, then make note of what you would add.

SAMPLE ARTIFACT
Ryan Bookler
Lesson Plan

<u>Subject</u>: Social Studies

<u>Grade Level</u>: Third

<u>Background</u>: Students have no knowledge of Sim Town. However, they should have an idea what is in the town of Aurora and how it works. By using Sim Town, students will be able to explore and test new ideas; they discover what happens when principles are applied to a situation, rather than merely learn about a set of facts and principles.

<u>Students</u>: There are about 24 students in the class. Most are well-behaved, but there are a few exceptions. Dijon, Clarence, and Donnie are disruptive in class. The ability levels differ in the class.

<u>Objectives</u>:
- Create and manage their own town
- Design their town's layout
- Design street networks and neighborhoods
- Determine how their town will grow
- Students will become explorers that create and follow their own hypotheses.

<u>Anticipatory Set</u>:
- What town do you live in?
- Do you have friends or family members who live in other towns?
- What towns do they live in?
- What kinds of things are in these towns?
- What you are going to do today is build your own town.

<u>Methods, Procedures, Activities</u>:
1) Go to computer
2) Click on New Town
3) Type name of town. Mr. Ryan's Town.
4) So I want to build my own town. How might I attract people to my town?
5) First, I need to get the people to come.
6) How would they get to my town?
7) Once the people get to town, where would they stay?
8) So, we want to build houses.
9) Now that they live at my town, how are they going to get money?
10) Where can they work?
11) What happens if their home starts on fire? Fire Department.
12) Who will keep us safe from bad people?
13) Where do we put the bad people?
14) What happens if we want to write a letter?
15) Show kids the bulldozer tool.
16) Show kids how they can design a character.
17) Show kids the Homes-to-Business Balance.
18) Use the magnifying glass.
19) Show kids the Natural Resources button.
20) Show kids the Newspaper button.
21) Tell the kids to work at a computer with the person next to them. We will switch in fifteen minutes.
22) Tell the kids to put their red cup up when they have built a road, house, and a business.

<u>Modeling</u>: I will show the children some of the features when I explain it to them using the computer.

<u>Checks for Understanding</u>: Did the students raise their hand when they built a road, house, and business?

<u>Materials List</u>:
-Sim Town
-Computers
-T.V. screen

<u>Guided Practice</u>:
I will be walking around to help the students when needed.

<u>Evaluation</u>:
Did the students understand how to work the program?
Were they frustrated?

> Closure: Let the students know that they will be able to work on Sim Town another day.
>
> Requests for feedback from observer:
> Did I speak clearly?
> What could I have done better?
> What was good about my lesson?

SAMPLE ARTIFACT
Ryan Bookler
Clinical Experience Reflection

…During my clinical, I gave a lesson on Sim Town (it is like Sim City) and a lesson on fractions using Hershey candy bars. The Sim Town lesson went real well. The kids understood what I was saying and were excited about the activity. Mr. Burrows, my clinical teacher, offered me some suggestions. He told me not to use slang such as "goin'" or "comin'". When giving directions to the students, I should ask them to repeat what I said. Therefore, I will know if they understand me. The fraction lesson did not go as well. The problems I gave the class were too hard and I did not explain everything clearly. Part of the problem was me being nervous. Using the Hershey candy bars was a good idea, but they were starting to melt even after they had been in the freezer for a couple of days. I learned not to put a Hershey bar on the overhead because it melted real quickly. The higher level kids were able to understand the lesson, but the lower kids were lost.

…Overall, I enjoyed my experience in Mrs. Churchill's class. I did learn many new things, including to appreciate Mrs. Churchill. She gave me several good ideas to use in my classroom. When I was giving my lesson, some kids were raising their hands while others were shouting out the answers. After my lesson, I asked Mrs. Churchill what I could have done to prevent this from happening. She said, "Call on the students who raise their hands and then thank them for raising their hand." I did this for the next lesson I taught and it worked great. All of the kids raised their hands and did not shout out answers. This was one of the many positive learning experiences that I will emulate in my classroom someday.

Ryan frankly and humorously addresses matters of practicality with the candy bars, modeling appropriate grammar, and classroom management; however, as always, there are possible additions and changes. Ryan does not reflect on how he could have changed the lesson itself.

- How did the previously mentioned disruptive children behave? What modifications did he make to help them to succeed?
- Were all the students computer literate? If not, how did he address this?
- Ryan mentions the red cups for students to put up when they have created a road, house, or business, but the red cup is not included in materials needed or in his checks for understanding.
- Finally, Ryan's understanding of guided practice, evaluation, and closure needs work. It is possible that his supervisor was not yet looking for Ryan's mastery in these areas. For future reference, however, guided practice includes walking the students

- through the lesson as the teacher models it. The evaluation should have addressed some of the stated objectives, and how he could tell whether those objectives had been met. And last, closure entails taking time to review the lesson, ask for feedback, lead students to think about how they learned (metacognition), and plan for next time.

Our last lesson plan artifact is by Stephanie, a returning adult student. Again, take notes on what you would change as you read Stephanie's lesson, then read the suggestions following the lesson.

SAMPLE ARTIFACT
Stephanie Leonard
Vocabulary Lesson
November 18, 1999

Reading Content: Vocabulary

Time: 10-29 minutes

Reading Background: Students should have a background in phonics. Students should know how to compose a sentence.

Objectives: Students will be able to:
- Read and write the vocabulary words for The Patchwork Quilt.
- Use the vocabulary words properly in a sentence.
- Identify the words when reading The Patchwork Quilt.

Materials: Students—crayons or markers, reading book, paper, pencil. Teacher—construction paper, prepared paper quilt squares, sticky tack or tape, list of vocabulary words on an overhead transparency, vocabulary words on index cards.

Grouping of Students: Pairs or groups of three, if needed.

Preparation: Students will have previewed the story, The Patchwork Quilt. Once students have divided into groups, instruct the students to get out a blank piece of paper and a pencil.

Instructions for Teachers:
1) Begin by reading the list of vocabulary words to the students. Provide a definition for each word. Use the word in a sentence.
2) Have students write each word on their pieces of paper with no regard to spelling. Then, display the list on an overhead for the students to see the words and correct any spelling mistakes.
3) Next, assign a word to each group of students. Have the words written on index cards and let each group pick one card.

---

4) Hand out a piece of construction paper to each group of students. Have students place the construction paper in the vertical position. Remind students that vertical is long and tall like a <u>v</u>ase.

5) Instruct the student on the left of each pair that he/she will write the vocabulary word in the top half of the construction paper with a marker or crayon in his/her best handwriting.

6) Instruct the student on the right of each pair that he/she will write a sentence using the vocabulary word in the bottom half of the construction paper with a marker or crayon in his/her best handwriting. Have students underline the vocabulary word in the sentence.

7) Instruct the students, if they do not remember the definition of the word they are using, to use the glossary in the back of their reading books to find the definition.

8) When everyone is finished, place one of the prepared quilt squares with sticky tack or tape on the top of the blackboard or a wall. Have the first group bring its completed vocabulary quilt square to the front of the room. Have one student read the word and the other student read the sentence. Place this square next to the prepared quilt square. Place another prepared quilt square next to the vocabulary quilt square and continue until all groups have finished.

9) Remember to distribute the squares evenly according to the number of groups. Use prepared quilt squares to fill in any uneven parts at the end.

10) Finish by using choral reading of each vocabulary word of the vocabulary quilt.

Evaluation: Did the students use the vocabulary word properly in a sentence? Did the students follow directions for making their vocabulary quilt squares?

Closure:
1) Instruct students to look for vocabulary words when re-reading the story.
2) Ask the students if they have any questions.

Additional: This lesson can be done using smaller pieces of paper. After the lesson is done, the words can be added to a word wall, if one is present in the classroom.

What's Missing?

One error is the omission of the correct citation of the book used. Another important piece of information omitted is the grade level of the students. Some suggested modifications that Stephanie could have included are:

- Allow students with disabilities in written expression to dictate their sentences.
- Rather than have a third group member go without a job to do, Stephanie could work with that left-over student as her partner.
- Stephanie may wish to allow more than 10-20 minutes for this lesson so that students have the time to be neat and creative. Also, some students panic when given time limits and are then incapable of focusing on the task at hand.

- It would be wise to mention how she would monitor comprehension of the instructions by asking students to repeat the instructions and by circulating the room as students worked.

The following thoughts are from Ginger Law, a classroom aide in a self-contained class for middle school students with behavior disorders. Ginger is in the dual position of having the opportunity to use her parenting skills in the classroom and her teaching skills in her home. As an aide working with students with behavior disorders and learning disabilities, Ginger must be able to implement modifications. As a parent of a student with learning disabilities, Ginger must also know what modifications to ask for and to expect.

As a teacher's assistant in a classroom for students with behavior disorders, I use many modifications. Most of the students have learning disabilities as well as behavior problems. Dictation is used to help the students with power writing, when they are given the opportunity to think aloud without worrying about getting the ideas on paper, it gives them a boost in their thinking process. At times the work is lessened. Or, with multiple choice question tests or worksheets, the number of choices are cut down. Another important modification that is implemented is allowing extended time to turn in their work. Some students do below grade level work. If the student has visual problems, large-type print books are used; and if none are available, then enlarged copies of text are made. The most often used modification is to either read to the student or use audio tapes.

Being in this position has benefited me to help my own child that has learning disabilities. I know what modifications that I can request on his IEP that will ensure him to succeed in the classroom. The modifications he has access to are audio and/or video tapes, having tests read to him, being allowed to dictate responses, and having extended time.

I expect the teachers who work with my child to know what modifications that he can use and to implement them. As a teacher's assistant, I believe that you should use whatever modifications are needed to prevent stress (for both the student and the teacher) and to promote self-esteem. But most importantly, I believe that parent-teacher contact is vital in order for the student and the teacher to be successful.

--Ginger Law, paraprofessional and parent

The implications of Ginger's thoughts are paramount to you. Whether you are getting your degree in regular education or special education, you must be aware of the need for modifications and also be skilled at both creating and implementing them. Parents like Ginger may be included as part of the interview team. Additionally administrators[2]

---

[2] For more information on national standards related to meeting diverse learning needs, see the Appendix.

always look for teachers who are willing to use a variety of methods to teach and to assess students with diverse learning needs. Remember, the willingness to modify instruction and assessment is also a very pro-active classroom management technique.[3]

In your notes, take a moment to write down modifications that you have received or observed, wished that you or someone else could have, or have either implemented or would like to try.[4]

Curricular Modifications

More and more, students with mild, moderate, or severe learning or behavioral disabilities are receiving their instruction in an age-appropriate regular education environment. Inclusion and regular education initiative (REI) are two terms for such an instructional delivery model. Inclusion and REI students are believed by their teachers and parents to benefit socially and academically from being around peers who have not been identified as disabled.

One important facet of being an educator is striving to create meaningful lessons that are accessible to students of different abilities and varying backgrounds. In the best case scenarios, you will have an expert in the field of special education to help you to ensure this worthy goal. Unfortunately, money and space sometimes preclude the possibility of assigning two certified instructors to one group of students. In these cases, you may or may not have an aide/paraprofessional at your disposal, and the certified special educator may be able to make only scheduled appearances. Therefore, whenever you write lesson plans, it is wise to include your ideas for curricular modifications. Whether or not a student is legally labeled as having a learning need with an Individual Education Plan (IEP), there will always be students who may benefit from either receiving alternate forms of instruction or from being allowed alternate ways of showing comprehension.

Friend and Bursuck (1996) offer some suggestions for those times when you are at a loss for ideas and do not know where to turn. They suggest joining a professional organization such as the Council for Exceptional Children[5], forming a teacher support group, or checking out the supplemental, modifying materials at your local teacher supply store (Friend & Bursuck, 1996).

---

[3] For other pro-active classroom management techniques to consider mentioning in your portfolio, see chapter 7 on classroom management.

[4] For information on how to articulate your modification ideas, see the Modifications checklists included in the Appendix.

[5] See Appendix A for Key Professional Organizations.

Curricular Modification Artifacts

If you create your own list of possible modifications, you may wish to also include samples of the curriculum before and after the modifications have been made. Another idea is to divide your modifications list into learning modalities or into forms of presentation. If you use a learning modalities approach, use headings such as:

- Auditory
- Visual
- Kinesthetic
- Tactile

For a list of presentation and performance demand modifications, consider using headings such as:

- Lecture
- Seating
- Printed materials
- Auditory aids
- Visual aids
- Note-taking
- Overhead projector
- Computer presentation
- Lighting
- Chalkboard/White board
- Peer study buddy
- Calculator
- Word processor
- Translation/interpreting

The following list of possible modifications was brainstormed by a group of students in a developmental reading course. If you include previously published lists of modifications in your portfolio, be sure to cite your references.

MODIFICATIONS FOR SPECIAL NEEDS

preferential seating

work in pairs or groups

dictation

manipulatives

oral tests & assignments

extra time

technology

hands-on activities

calculators

mixed groups

word processors

change materials to fit goals

choices

offer challenges at all levels

multiple choice spelling tests

variety of assessment tools

literature response journals

pre-tests

alternate forms of work

role plays

talk directly to hearing impaired

overheads & other vis. aids

students tape record answers

reduce size of task

books printed in Braille

larger print

Another impressive artifact is this revising and editing worksheet created by Kelly Sanders, a student at Northern Illinois University. This graphic organizer will help students organize their thoughts and can be used by students of any ability level.

Revising and Editing Worksheet

Title of Paper:_____

Written By:_____

Revised and Edited By:_____

<table>
<tr><td>Positive Areas of Content:</td><td>Negative Areas of Content:</td></tr>
</table>

Positive Areas of Content: Negative Areas of Content:
1.

2.

3.

4.

5.

6.

7.

Changes Needed in Spelling, Punctuation, and Grammar:
1.

2.

3.

My favorite part of _____'s story is

_____
_____
_____
_____.

Implications

Competent, caring teachers create lesson plans to engage all types of students in their classes. Their lessons reflect well-thought out strategies, and encompass the principles of a particular model of teaching. Curricular modifications are necessary, wise to use, insightful, and compassionate.

References

Friend, M. & Bursuck, W. (1996). Including Students With Special Needs. Boston: Allyn & Bacon.

Hunter, M. & Russell, D. (1981). Increasing Your Teaching Effectiveness. Palo Alto, CA: The Learning Institute.

Website Suggestions

To find out how regular educators and adapted physical education specialists can creatively and meaningfully include students of all ages and abilities in regular physical education programs without making complex curricular changes or costly staff additions, go to
http://www.amazon.com/exec/obidos/ISBN=1557661561/specialink...

"Why Math, Why Me?" is a website created in an effort to offer elementary teachers (general and special education) a resource where they can gather information about effective ways to teach math to students who are currently not successful due to lack of interest, low motivation, learning disabilities, environmental factors, etc. Go to
http://www.ionet.net/~terriv/

To find answers to the question, "What Are ADAPTATIONS, ACCOMMODATIONS and MODIFICATIONS," go to
http://at-advocacy.phillynews.com/data/modsaccomdef.html

For a list of websites which focus on issues relating to diversity and inclusion, go to
http://scrtec.org/track/tracks/s02326.html

NOTES

_____

_____

_____

_____

_____

_____

_____

_____

_____

_____

_____

_____

_____

_____

_____

_____

A Final Note

By now you've learned what teaching portfolios are, several reasons to create them, and what types of styles are possible. You've read advice from principals and parents. You've seen examples of a wide variety of artifacts, and you should have a good idea of just what you plan to include in your own portfolio.

As you create your own portfolio, keep the following suggestions in mind:

- Determine just what characteristics about yourself you want your portfolio to convey. Make sure you've included the artifacts that will present you in this desired way.
- When your portfolio is done, have several different people examine your portfolio and tell you what it tells them about you—are the characteristics you wished to convey coming through?
- Research the school districts you'll be applying to, and arrange your portfolio to meet the goals, standards, and values of those districts.
- If you base your portfolio on a specific set of standards, make that clear—cite the organization responsible for the standards, why you chose them as your focus, and then list the standards themselves.
- Practice presenting your portfolio over and over. Have friends randomly choose a topic, and see how fluently you can turn to the artifacts addressing that topic.
- Have friends tell you whether or not your portfolio is "user-friendly." Is the table of contents helpful? Did you color-code or tab your artifacts? What devices have you included to make your portfolio easy to use?

Thank you for taking the time to use this text. I am interested in hearing how your own experiences with portfolios turn out, and I am available to offer suggestions, encouragement, or even commiseration. Email me at:
mrspatty1@juno.com

Best wishes,
Patricia L. Rieman

APPENDIX A:
KEY
PROFESSIONAL
ORGANIZATIONS

It is impossible to list every possible professional organization in the field of education, however, there are several that any new teacher should be familiar with.

American Alliance for Health, Physical Education, Recreation and Dance (AAHPERD)
1900 Association Dr., Reston, VA 22091 (703) 476-3400
www.aahperd.org

Association for Supervision and Curriculum Development (ASCD)
1250 N. Pitt St., Alexandria, VA 22314-1403 (703) 549-9110
www.ascd.org/

Council for Exceptional Children (CEC)
1920 Association Dr., Reston, VA 22091-1589 (703) 620-3660
www.cec.spd.org

Distributive Education Clubs of America (DECA)
1908 Association Dr., Reston, VA 22091 (703) 860-5000
http://www.wadeca.org/

International Reading Association (IRA)
800 Barksdale Rd., PO Box 8139, Newark, DE 19714-8139
(302) 731-1600
www.ira.org

Junior Achievement
1 Education Way, Colorado Springs, CO 80906 (719) 540-8000
www.ja.org

Music Teachers National Association (MTNA)
617 Vine St., Ste. 1432, Cincinnati, OH 45202 (513) 421-1420
http://www.mtna.org/

National Art Education Association (NAEA)
1916 Association Dr., Reston, VA 22091-1590 (703) 860-8000
http://www.naea-reston.org/

National Council for the Social Studies (NCSS)
3501 Newark St. NW, Washington, DC 20016 (202) 966-7840
www.ncss.org

National Council of Teachers of English (NCTE)
1111 Kenyon Rd., Urbana, IL 61801 (217) 328-3870
www.ncte.org

National Council of Teachers of Mathematics (NCTM)
1906 Association Dr., Reston, VA 22091-1593 (703) 620-9840

www.nctm.org

National FFA Organization (NFFAO)
National FFA Center, Box 15160
5632 Mt. Vernon Memorial Hwy, Alexandria, VA 22309-0160
(703) 360-3600

www.agriculture.com

National Middle School Association (NMSA)
4807 Evanswood Dr., Columbus, OH 43229 (614) 848-8211

www.nmsa.org

National Science Teachers Association (NSTA)
1742 Connecticut Ave. NW, Washington, DC 20009-1171
(202) 328-5800

www.nsta.org

Teachers of English to Speakers of Other Languages (TESOL)
1600 Cameron St., Ste. 300, Alexandria, VA 22314-2751
(703) 836-0774

www.tesol.edu/

Technology Student Association (TSA)
1914 Association Dr., Reston, VA 22091 (703) 860-9000

http://www.tsawww.org/

APPENDIX B:
STATE
DEPARTMENTS
OF
EDUCATION

Alabama Dept. of Education
Gordon Persons Office Building
50 North Ripley St.
Montgomery, AL 36130-3901
(205) 242-9977

www.alsde.edu

Alaska Dept. of Education
P.O. Box F
801 W. 10th St., Ste. 200
Juneau, AK 99801-1894
(907) 465-2810

www.educ.state.ak.us

Arizona Dept. of Public Instruction
P.O. Box 25609
1535 W. Jefferson
Phoenix, AZ 85002
(602) 542-4368

http://ade.state.az.us

Arkansas Dept. of Education
4 State Capitol Mall
Little Rock, AR 72201-1071
(501) 682-4342

http://arkedu.ik12.ar.us/

California Dept. of Education
721 Capitol Mall
Sacramento, CA 95814
(916) 657-5485
http://goldmine.cde.ca.gov

Colorado Dept. of Education
210 E. Colfax Ave.
Denver, CO 80203
(303) 866-6628

www.cde.state.co.us

Connecticut Dept. of Education
Box 2219
Hartford, CT 06145-2219
(203) 566-5201

www.aces.k12.ct.us/csdf

Delaware Dept. of Public Instruction
P.O. Box 1402, Townsend Bldg. #279
Federal and Lockeman Streets
Dover, DE 19903
(302) 739-4688

www.dpi.state.de.us

**District of Columbia, Division of State
Services Teacher Education**
415 12th St., NW, Room 1013
Washington, DC 20004
(202) 724-4246

www.k12.dc.us

Florida Dept. of Education
Room PL 08, Capitol Building
Tallahassee, FL 32301
(904) 487-1785

www.firn.edu/doe

Georgia Dept. of Education
2066 Twin Towers East
Atlanta, GA 30334-5020
(404) 657-9000

www.doe.k12.ga.us

Hawaii Dept. of Education
P.O. Box 2360
Honolulu, HI 96804
(808) 586-3420

www.K12.hi.us

Idaho Dept. of Education
L.B. Jordan Office Building
650 W. State St.
Boise, ID 83720-3650

www.sde.state.id.us

Illinois Board of Education
100 North 1st St.
Springfield, IL 62777
(217) 782-4321

www.isbe.state.il.us

Indiana Dept. of Education
Room 229, State House
Indianapolis, IN 46204-2798
(317) 232-6665

www.doe.state.in.us

Iowa Dept. of Education
Grimes State Office Building
East 14th and Grand Streets
Des Moines, IA 50319-0147
(515) 281-3245

www.state.ia.us/educate

Kansas Dept. of Education
Kansas State Education Building
120 East 10th St.
Topeka, KS 66612-1182
(913) 296-2288

www.ksbe.state.ks.us

Kentucky Dept. of Education
18th Floor-Capital Plaza Tower
500 Mero Street
Frankfort, KY 40601
(502) 564-4606

www.kde.state.ky.us

Louisiana Dept. of Education
P.O. Box 94064
Baton Rouge, LA 70804-9064
(504) 342-3490

www.doe.state.la.us

Maine Dept. of Education
State House Stat. 23
Augusta, ME 04333
(207) 287-5944

**www.state.me.us/education/homepage.
htm**

Maryland Dept. of Education
200 W. Baltimore St.
Baltimore, MD 20201
(301) 333-2142

http://sailor.lib.md.us/msde

Michigan Dept. of Education
P.O. Box 30008
Lansing, MI 48909
(517) 373-3310

www.mde.state.mi.us

Minnesota Dept. of Education
616 Capitol Square Building
St. Paul, MN 55101
(612) 296-2046

www.educ.state.mn.us

Mississippi Dept. of Education
Box 771
550 High Street
Jackson, MS 39205-0771
(601) 359-3483

http://mdek12.state.ms.us

**Missouri Dept. of Elementary and
Secondary Education**
P.O. Box 480
205 Jefferson St.
Jefferson City, MO 65102
(314) 751-0051

http://services.dese.state.mo.us

Montana Office of Public Instruction
P.O. Box 202501
106 State Capitol
Helena, MT 59620-2501
(406) 444-3150

http://161.7.114.15/OPI/OPIHTML

Nebraska Dept. of Education
301 Centennial Mall South
Box 94987
Lincoln, NE 68509-4987
(800) 371-4642

www.NDE.State.NE.US

Nevada Dept. of Education
1850 E. Sahara, Ste. 200
Las Vegas, NV 89158
(702) 386-5401

http://www.state.nv.us/

New Hampshire Dept. of Education
101 Pleasant St., State Office Park South
Concord, NH 03301
(603) 271-2407

www.state.nh.us/doe/education.html

New Jersey Dept. of Education
CN 503
Trenton, NJ 08625-0503
(609) 292-2070

www.state.nj.us/education

New Mexico Dept. of Education
Education Building
300 Don Gaspar
Santa Fe, NM 87501-2786
(505) 827-6587

http://sde.state.nm.us

New York Office of Teaching
Room 5A11-CEC
State Education Department
Albany, NY 12230
(518) 474-3901

www.nysed.gov

North Carolina Dept. of Public Instruction
301 N. Wilmington St.
Raleigh, NC 27601-2825
(919) 733-4125

www.dpi.state.nc.us

North Dakota Dept. of Public Instruction
State Capitol Building, 11th Floor
600 Boulevard Ave. East
Bismarck, ND 58505-0440
(701) 224-2264

www.sendit.nodak.edu/dpi

Ohio Dept. of Education
65 S. Front St., Rm. 1012
Columbus, OH 43266-0308
(614) 466-3593

www.ode.ohio.gov

Oklahoma Prof. Standards Dept.of Education
Oliver Hodge Mem. Education Bldg.
2500 N. Lincoln Blvd., Rm. 211
Oklahoma City, OK 73105-4599
(405) 521-3337

www.sde.state.ok.us

Oregon Dept. of Education
700 Pringle Parkway, SE
Salem, OR 97310-0290
(503) 378-3573

www.state.or.us

Pennsylvania Dept. of Education
333 Market St., 10th Floor
Harrisburg, PA 17126-0333
(717) 787-2967

www.cas.psu.edu/pde.html

Rhode Island Dept. of Education
22 Hayes Street
Providence, RI 02908
(401) 277-2675

http://www.ridoe.net

South Carolina Dept. of Education
10006 Rutledge Bldg.
1429 Senate St.
Columbia, SC 29201
(803) 734-8492

www.state.sc.us/sde

South Dakota Teacher Education and Certification Dept. of Education
700 Governors Drive
Pierre, SD 57501-2291
(605) 773-3553

www.state.sd.us

Tennessee Dept. of Education
100 Cordell Hull Building
Nashville, TN 37243-0375
(615) 741-2731

www.state.tn.us

Texas Education Agency
William B. Travis Building
1701 N. Congress Ave.
Austin, TX 78701-1494
(512) 463-8976

www.tea.texas.gov

Utah Office of Education
250 E. 500 South St.
Salt Lake City, UT 84111
(801) 538-7740

www.usoe.k12.ut.us

Vermont Dept. of Education
120 State St.
Montpelier, VT 05602-2703
(802) 828-2445

www.state.vt.us/educ

Virginia Dept. of Education
James Monroe Building
Fourteenth & Franklin Streets
P.O. Box 6-Q
Richmond, VA 23216-2120
(804) 225-2755

www.pen.k12.va.us

Washington Dept. of Public Instruction
Old Capitol Building
P.O. Box 47200
Olympia, WA 98504-7200
(206) 753-6773

www.ospi.wednet.edu

West Virginia Dept. of Education
Building 6, Room 337
1900 Kanawha Blvd., East
Charleston, WV 25305-0330
(800) 982-2378

http://access.k12.wv.us

Wisconsin Dept. of Public Instruction
Box 7841
125 South Webster St.
Madison, WI 53707-7841
(608) 266-1027

http://badger.state.wi.us/agencies/dpi

Wyoming Dept. of Education
2300 Capitol Avenue
Hathaway Bldg., 2nd Floor
Cheyenne, WY 82002
(307) 777-7291

www.k12.wy.us